The Student-Loan Catastrophe

The Student-Loan Catastrophe

POSTCARDS FROM THE RUBBLE

• • •

Richard Fossey

ISBN-13: 9781548591717
ISBN-10: 1548591718
Library of Congress Control Number: 2017910780
CreateSpace Independent Publishing Platform
North Charleston, South Carolina

It was like we had known all along that the sky was going to fall and then it fell and we pretended to be surprised.

—ELIN HILDERBRAND
THE LOVE SEASON

Table of Contents

The Student-Loan Bubble is Eerily Similar to the Home-Mortgage Crisis

• • •

A FEW MONTHS AGO, STEVE Rhode posted a thought-provoking blog titled "The Student Loan Bubble That Many Don't Want to See."[1] He argued that student-loan indebtedness is in a bubble that will soon burst, creating two huge problems: First, when the student-loan market collapses, postsecondary education will be out of reach for most people, which will "put a drag on the overall economy as fewer and fewer people will be able to pay for tuition that outpaces inflation." Second, a sharp contraction in federal student-loan revenue along with a shrinking student base will force many colleges to cut tuition, putting them under enormous financial stress. Rhode predicts that "many schools, public and private, will fail."

Mr. Rhode sees a parallel between the student-loan program and the overheated housing market that led to a global financial crisis in 2008. Just as financiers packaged home mortgages into asset-backed securities called ABSs, the banks have bundled student loans into so-called SLABS, or student-loan asset-backed securities.

The home-mortgage market went into free fall when investors woke up to the fact that the ratings services (Moody's, Fitch, etc.) had rated ABSs as investment grade when in fact, a lot of them were

---

1 Steve Rhode, "The Student Loan Bubble That Many Don't Want to See," *Get Out Of Debt Guy* (blog), July 15, 2016, accessed August 5, 2017, https://getoutofdebt.org/99519/student-loan-bubble-many-dont-want-see.

junk because they were packed with mortgages that were headed for default.[2]

Now we see Moody's and Fitch downgrading SLABS based on the fact that student borrowers are not paying off their loans as investors expected.[3] More than 5 million borrowers have signed up for income-driven repayment plans (IDRs) that lower monthly loan payments and stretch out the repayment period from ten years to twenty or even twenty-five years. SLABS investors now don't know when or how much they are going to be paid on their investments.

Some policy commentators reject the notion that the student-loan market is in a bubble. In a book published last year, Beth Akers and Matthew M. Chingos wrote, "Student loans have a zero chance of becoming the next housing crisis because the market is too small and essentially functions as a government program rather than a market."[4] Akers and Chingos point out that student debt represents only 10 percent of overall consumer debt while home mortgages accounts for 70 percent of household indebtedness.

Personally, I think Steve Rhode is right: higher education is sustained by a student-loan bubble that the nation's colleges and universities refuse to see. In fact, there are eerie similarities between the housing market before it crashed in 2008 and the current level of student-loan indebtedness.

First, tuition at many colleges and universities is wildly overpriced, just as the housing market was overpriced in the early 2000s.

---

2 "Big Three credit raters tighten their grip after ducking reform," *American Banker* (blog), August 2, 2017, accessed August 5, 2017, https://www.americanbanker. com/articles/big-three-credit-raters-tighten-their-grip-after-ducking-reform.

3 Annamaria Andriotis, "Debt Relief for Students Snarls Market for Their Loans," *Wall Street Journal*, September 23, 2015, accessed August 3, 2017, https://www.wsj. com/articles/debt-relief-is-snarling-the-market-for-student-loans-1443035071.

4 Beth Akers and Matthew Chingos, *Game of Loans: The Rhetoric and Reality of Student Debt* (Princeton, NJ: Princeton University Press, 2016).

This is particularly true in the for-profit sector and at private liberal-arts colleges.

As has been widely reported, liberal-arts colleges are now discounting tuition for freshman students by almost 50 percent—a clear sign that their posted tuition prices are too high.[5] And for-profit colleges are seeing enrollment declines. The University of Phoenix, for example, saw its enrollments drop by about half over a period of five years.[6]

Second, the monitoring agencies for both markets failed to do their jobs. As illustrated in the movie *The Big Short*, the financial ratings agencies rated mortgage-backed securities as investment grade when in fact, those bundled mortgages included a lot of subprime mortgages.

Likewise, the Department of Education (DOE) reports three-year default rates for student loans that vastly understates how many student borrowers are failing to pay back their loans. The DOE recently reported that about 10 percent of the most recent cohort of student borrowers defaulted within three years. But the five-year default rate is 28 percent, and the five-year default rate for a recent cohort of students who attended for-profit schools is a shocking 47 percent.[7]

---

5 Kellie Woodhouse, "Discounting Grows Again," *Inside Higher Ed*, August 25, 2015, accessed August 3, 2017, https://www.insidehighered.com/news/2015/08/25/tuition-discounting-grows-private-colleges-and-universities.

6 Patrick Gillespie, "University of Phoenix Has Lost Half Its Students," *CNN Money*, March 25, 2015, accessed August 3, 2017, http://money.cnn.com/2015/03/25/investing/university-of-phoenix-apollo-earnings-tank/.

7 Adam Looney and Constantine Yannelis, *A Crisis in Student Loans? How Changes in the Characteristics of Borrowers and in the Institutions They Attended Contributed to Rising Default Rates* (Washington, DC: Brookings Institution, 2015), https://www.brookings.edu/bpea-articles/a-crisis-in-student-loans-how-changes-in-the-characteristics-of-borrowers-and-in-the-institutions-they-attended-contributed-to-rising-loan-defaults/.

And of course, the government's vigorous effort to get distressed student borrowers into IDRs also helps hide the true default rate. A high percentage of people who enter IDRs are making loan payments so low that they will never pay off their loans.

In short, Steve Rhode's analysis is correct. A rising level of student-loan debt has created a bubble, and the bubble is going to burst. Colleges raised tuition prices far above the nation's inflation rate, knowing that students will simply take out larger student loans to pay their tuition bills. Millions of Americans paid too much for their postsecondary educations and can't pay back their loans.

So far, the DOE has hidden the magnitude of this crisis, but the game will soon be up. Colleges are closing at an accelerating rate, stock prices for publicly traded for-profit colleges are down, and long-term default rates are shockingly high.[8]

It is true, as Akers and Chingos pointed out, that the student-loan market is not nearly as large as the home-mortgage market was when it crashed in 2008. But Akers and Chingos fail to acknowledge the enormous human cost that has been imposed on millions of Americans who took out student loans in the hope of getting an education that would lead to a better life.

Instead, the only thing many Americans got by taking out student loans is an enormous debt load that they can't pay off or discharge in bankruptcy. Eight million Americans have defaulted on their student loans, 5.6 million are in IDRs that stretch their payment obligations out for as long as twenty-five years, and millions more are playing for time by putting their loans in forbearance or deferment.

---

8 Amy Thielen, "Declines at For-Profit Colleges Take a Big Toll on Their Stocks," *The Street*, May 8, 2015, accessed August 3, 2017, https://www.thestreet.com/story/13144238/1/decline-in-for-profit-colleges-takes-a-big-toll-on-their-stocks.html.

Snapshot of the Student-Loan Crisis from a Recent New York Federal Reserve Bank Report: Surprise, Surprise! Debt Levels Are Rising

• • •

RESEARCHERS AT THE NEW YORK Federal Reserve Bank issued a press release on April 3, 2017 that reported on household borrowing and student debt. Here are some excerpts from that press release. I have italicized particularly interesting passages:

STUDENT-LOAN UPDATE

Aggregate student-loan balances have continued to increase and stood at about $1.3 trillion at the end of 2016, an increase of about 170 percent from 2006. Aggregate student debt is increasing because more students are taking out loans, the loans are for larger amounts, and the speed with which borrowers repay their debts has slowed down. *New debt originations continue to increase: 2015 graduates with student loans left school with about $34,000, up from only $20,000 just ten years before.*

While about 36 percent of student debt holders owed less than $10,000, and 65 percent owed less than $25,000, only about 5 percent of student debt holders owed more than $100,000 in debt in 2016. *Yet these big-balance borrowers account for nearly 30 percent of the total balances outstanding, so their outcomes and repayment success have a disproportionate influence on the overall picture.*

Student-loan default and delinquency rates appear to have leveled off, albeit at a relatively high level. Defaults peaked in 2012, and have stabilized since 2013; the 2009–11 cohorts saw the highest default rates, with some improvement among more recent cohorts.

We have noted in the past that delinquency and default rates are lower among higher-balance borrowers; however, the default rates among higher-balance borrowers have worsened notably in recent years. Further, payment progress is slower among those who borrowed more. Ten years later, over 70 percent of the original balance has been repaid among those who had borrowed less than $5,000 when they left college in 2006, compared to a reduction of only 25 percent among students who borrowed more than $100,000.

Higher balances, increasing participation in student-loan programs, and slower repayment are pushing up aggregate student-loan balances. Although defaults are improving, the pay down progress of recent cohorts continues to decline.[1]

The Fed researchers also commented on the relationship between student-loan indebtedness and homeownership:

HOMEOWNERSHIP

The final portion of the press briefing was on educational attainment, student loans, and homeownership, using

---

1 Rajashri Chakrabarti et al., "At the N.Y. Fed: Press Briefing on Household Borrowing with Close-Up on Student Debt," *Liberty Street Economics* (blog), April 3, 2017 (italics supplied), accessed August 3, 2017, http://libertystreeteconomics.newyorkfed.org/2017/04/at-the-ny-fed-press-briefing-on-household-borrowing-with-close-up-on-student-debt.html.

education records from the National Student Clearinghouse that were newly matched with credit records from the Consumer Credit Panel. These findings are presented in greater detail in a separate post. New analysis shows that college education is associated with markedly higher homeownership rates regardless of debt status, which increases at each additional level of college attainment. *However, having student loans dampens homeownership rates at every level of education, and higher debt balances are associated with even lower homeownership rates.*[2]

In essence, the Federal Reserve Bank researchers are telling us this: loan balances are going up, more people are taking out student loans, and repayment rates are slowing, particularly for borrowers with high loan balances. I imagine a lot of these slow-paying borrowers are in the public service loan forgiveness (PSLF) program or an IDR.

The vast majority of people making payments under PSLF and IDR plans are not making payments large enough to pay down their loan balances. And, as the Fed researchers noted, among people who borrowed $100,000 or more, only 25 percent were able to pay off their student loans within ten years.

Regarding student loans and home buying, the Fed researchers had this to say: homeownership increases with people's education level, but student loans hamper the ability of people to buy a house, regardless of income level.[3]

---

2 Ibid.
3 Ibid.

Student-Loan Defaulters: Not All of Them Are Young

• • •

WHAT IS YOUR IMAGE OF the typical person who defaults on a college student loan? Do you envision a young and irresponsible college graduate—someone who ripped off the federal student-loan program by borrowing money to get a fancy college degree and then refused to pay it back? If so, your image would be inaccurate. A great many defaulters are from low-income families. Often, they attended a for-profit institution that provided them with little value. And—this may come as a surprise—many student-loan defaulters are not young.

Researchers for the Federal Reserve Bank of New York examined the loan statuses of 37 million student-loan borrowers in a 2012 report. Fourteen percent of these borrowers—approximately 5.4 million people—have at least one past-due student-loan account. According to the Federal Reserve Bank's report, only about 25 percent of student-loan borrowers with past-due balances are under the age of thirty. Forty percent of the student-loan borrowers with payments in arrears are at least forty years old. Almost one delinquent borrower in six (17.7 percent) is fifty years old or older. And about 5 percent of the people who are behind on their student-loan payments are at least sixty years old.[1]

---

1 Meta Brown et al., "Grading Student Loans," *Liberty Street Economics* (blog), March 5, 2012, accessed August 5, 2017, http://libertystreeteconomics. newyorkfed.org/2012/03/grading-student-loans.html.

Why are so many people falling behind on their student loans in midlife or late in life? There are several explanations.

First, some of the older student-loan borrowers are people who borrowed money in midlife, expecting to increase their income potential. Then, due to a variety of life circumstances, these borrowers did not earn the income they expected. Maybe they became ill, lost their jobs, or were the victims of the recent economic downturn. As a consequence, some of these older student-loan borrowers fell behind on their loans.

Second, some of the nation's older delinquent borrowers obtained economic hardship deferments on their loans, which temporarily exempted them from making regular student-loan payments. For a majority of these people, interest continued to accrue on their loans during the deferment period, causing their loan balances to grow. Consequently, when these borrowers began making loan payments again after their deferments expired, they sometimes had swollen loan balances that they simply could not repay.

Finally, I suspect some of the older people who are behind on their student-loan payments are people who had previously elected to pay off their loans under the income-contingent repayment option, which extends the loan repayment period out to twenty-five years. For some older people, the prospect of making student-loan payments during their retirement years may have seemed too daunting, causing them to stop making payments on their loans.

Older people who default on their student loans receive no dispensation from their loan obligations due to their age. In fact, in *Lockhart v. United States* (2005), the Supreme Court ruled that a student-loan defaulter's Social Security checks can be garnished.[2] Thus, some elderly people who failed to pay back their student loans will face severe financial hardship if they are totally dependent on Social Security income during their so-called golden years.

---

2 Lockhart v. United States, 546 US 142, 126 S. Ct. 699 (2005).

Obviously, no one would recommend a government policy that would make it easier for people to default on their student loans. Nevertheless, garnishing the Social Security checks of elderly student-loan defaulters is an overly harsh measure. Congress needs to pass legislation that bars lenders and collection agencies from garnishing student-loan defaulters' Social Security checks.

Social-Security Offsets Imposed on Elderly Student-Loan Defaulters are Heartless and Pointless

• • •

You can be young without money but
you can't be old without it.

—Tennessee Williams

If you are in your late fifties or early sixties, you've probably obtained an estimate of how much Social Security income you will receive when you retire. Most retired Americans depend on their Social Security checks to provide a significant amount of their overall retirement income.

But if you defaulted on a student loan, you may not receive your full Social Security benefit. The government may deduct part of your Social Security income and apply the deduction to your unpaid student loans.

In December 2016, the US Government Accountability Office issued a lengthy report (eighty-two pages) on the government's Social Security offset activities. Here are some of the highlights:

In 2015, 173,000 Americans had their Social Security income offset due to defaulted student loans. This is a dramatic increase from

2002, when the government only applied offsets to 36,000 Social Security recipients.[1]

Some Social Security recipients whose income was offset lived below the federal poverty guideline and others dropped below the poverty level after their Social Security checks were reduced.[2] In fact, as Senator Elizabeth Warren emphasized in a recent press release, "Since 2004, the number of seniors whose Social Security benefits have been garnished below the poverty line increased from 8,300 to 67,300."[3]

More than 7 million people age fifty and older still owe on student loans, and 870,000 people age sixty-five and older have student-loan debt. Among student-loan borrowers age sixty-five and older, 37 percent are in default.[4]

The amount of money the government collects from Social Security offsets is small beer. The government only collected $171 million from Social Security offsets in 2015, about one eighth the amount Hillary Clinton raised for her 2016 presidential campaign ($1.4 billion).[5]

---

1 US Government Accountability Office, *Social Security Offsets: Improvement to Program Design Could Better Assist Older Student Borrowers with Obtaining Permitted Relief*, GAO-17-45, December 19, 2016, accessed August 5, 2017, https://www.gao.gov/products/GAO-17-45.

2 Ibid., 27.

3 "McCaskill-Warren GAO Report Shows Shocking Increase in Student Loan Debt among Seniors," December 20, 2016, accessed August 3, 2017, https://www.warren.senate.gov/?p=press_release&id=1331.

4 US Government Accountability Office, *Social Security Offsets: Improvement to Program Design Could Better Assist Older Student Borrowers with Obtaining Permitted Relief*, GAO-17-45, December 19, 2017, fig. 2, 10, accessed August 5, 2017, 17, https://www.gao.gov/products/GAO-17-45.

5 Anu Narayanswamy, Darla Cameron and Matea Gold, "How much money is behind each campaign?" *Washington Post*, February 1, 2017, accessed August 3, 2017, https://www.washingtonpost.com/graphics/politics/2016-election/campaign-finance/.

Most of the money collected from Social Security offsets went toward paying fees and accumulated interest. "Of the approximately $1.1 billion collected through Social Security offsets from fiscal year 2001 through 2015 from borrowers of all ages, about 71 percent was applied to fees and interest."[6]

The Government Accountability Office also reported that several hundred thousand people who have experienced Social Security offsets are totally disabled and entitled to have their student loans forgiven, but only a minority of these people have applied for loan forgiveness.[7] Commendably, the DOE has suspended offsets for people who are totally disabled, whether or not they applied for loan forgiveness. Unfortunately, the government treats the amount of the forgiven debt as taxable income.[8]

The GAO report is packed with additional information and findings, but the bottom line is this: the government is hectoring elderly and disabled student-loan defaulters even though the amount of money the government collects is a pittance. Most of the money collected goes toward paying down fees and accumulated interest and does not reduce the individual defaulters' loan balances.

In short, the DOE's Social Security offset practices are pointless. Elderly or disabled people who defaulted on their student loans and are surviving on their Social Security checks will never pay off their loans.

Sandy Baum, a widely renowned expert on student loans, recommended in her recent book that the government stop offsetting

---

6 US Government Accountability Office. *Social Security Offsets: Improvement to Program Design Could Better Assist Older Student Borrowers with Obtaining Permitted Relief,* GAO-17-14, December 19, 2016, accessed August 5, 2017, https://www.gao.gov/products/GAO-17-45.

7 Ibid., 31.

8 Ibid.

the Social Security checks of defaulted student-loan debtors.[9] Does anyone disagree?

In fact, the government's Social Security offset practices strike me as an administrative form of sadism—the bureaucratic equivalent of small children who joylessly tear the wings off of insects.

Senator Elizabeth Warren has called for an end to the practice of garnishing student-loan defaulters' Social Security checks.[10] Surely, she can gather legislative support for a law that bans this practice. If she can't get that done, then Senator Warren is not a very effective consumer advocate.

---

9 Sandy Baum, *Student Debt: Rhetoric and Realities of Higher Education Financing* (New York: Palgrave-MacMillan, 2016).

10 Press Release of Senator Elizabeth Warren, "McCaskill-Warren GAO Report Shows Shocking Increase in Student Loan Debt among Seniors," December 20, 2016, accessed August 3, 2017, https://www.warren.senate.gov/?p=press_release&id=1331.

The Government Loans Money to Students Who Don't Have a Prayer of Paying It Back

• • •

THE STUDENT-LOAN CRISIS HAS ONE root cause. Year after year, the government has been loaning billions of dollars to students under the federal student-loan program, and millions of recipients don't have a prayer of paying back their loans.

Who benefits? The higher-education industry, including the stock holders and equity funds that own private colleges and universities, has gotten this money.[1]

Conner v. US Department of Education, a 2016 federal court decision, illustrates the reckless manner in which the Department of Education distributes student-loan money.[2] Patricia Conner, a Michigan schoolteacher, took out twenty-six separate student loans over a period of fourteen years to pursue graduate education in three fields: education, business administration, and communications. By the time she filled for bankruptcy at age sixty-one, she had accumulated over $214,000 in student-loan debt. According to the federal

---

1 Robert Kelchen, "How much do for-profit colleges rely on federal funds?" *Brown Center Chalkboard* (blog) January 11, 2017, accessed August 6, 2017, https://www.brookings.edu/blog/brown-center-chalkboard/2017/01/11/how-much-do-for-profit-colleges-rely-on-federal-funds/.

2 Conner v. US Department of Education, Case No. 15-1-541, 2016 WL 1178264 (E. D. Mich. March 28, 2016).

court, Conner did not make a single voluntary payment on any of her loans.[3]

In her bankruptcy proceedings, Conner argued that her debt should be discharged under the Bankruptcy Code's undue hardship standard. She cited her advanced age as a factor that should weigh in her favor.

But a Michigan bankruptcy court refused to release Conner from her debt, and a federal district court upheld the bankruptcy court's opinion on appeal.[4] The district court ruled that Conner's age could not be a consideration since she borrowed the money in midlife knowing she would have to pay it back. The district court also pointed out that the bankruptcy court had ordered Conner to apply for an income-based repayment plan (IBR). Under such a plan, the district court noted, she would only have been obligated to pay $267 a month on her massive debt. Conner initially complied and filed out an IBR application. Later, however, she "cancelled her application and never established a repayment plan."[5] The court did not say how long she would be obligated to make payments under an IBR, but these plans generally stretch out for at least twenty years.

Let's assume Conner signed up for an IBR and began paying $267 a month on her $214,000 debt. Let's also assume that the interest rate on this debt was 6 percent. At 6 percent, interest on $214,000 amounts to more than $12,000 a year, but Conner would only be paying about $3,200 a year toward her student loans.

This means Conner's debt would be negatively amortizing under an IBR—getting larger every year instead of smaller. After making payments for one year under an IBR, Conner would owe $223,000. After the second year, she would owe around $233,000. After three

---

3 Ibid., *1.
4 Ibid., *3.
5 Ibid., *1.

years, Conner's debt would grow to about a quarter of a million dollars, even if she faithfully made every monthly loan payment.

Obviously, by the time Conner's hypothetical IBR comes to a conclusion in twenty or twenty-five years, she will owe substantially more than she borrowed, and she will be over eighty years old. In short, the government will never get back the money it loaned to Ms. Conner.

Who benefited from this arrangement? Wayne State University, where Conner took her graduate-level classes, got most of Conner's loan money, which it used to pay its instructors and administrators. But what did Wayne State provide Conner for all this cash? Apparently not much because Conner was still a schoolteacher when she filed for bankruptcy, which is what she would have been even if she hadn't borrowed all that money to go to graduate school.

In my view, the Conner story is illustrative of the federal government's reckless student-loan program. The Department of Education is pumping billions of dollars a year into the corpulent higher-education industry, and it is getting only about half of it back. Moreover, in far too many cases, the students who are borrowing all this money aren't getting much value.

How long can this go on? I don't know, but it can't go on forever.

Student Loans, Bankruptcy, and Creditors' Lawyers: If Auschwitz Comes to the United States, Will Attorneys Handle the Paperwork?

• • •

I WAS A CHILD WHEN I learned about the Nazi concentration camps. I was a voracious reader when I was young, and I often wandered around our town library, browsing through the books. One day, I pulled a book off a shelf because I was intrigued by the title, and the pages fell open to a photo of one of the German concentration camps. It might have been Auschwitz, but I don't remember.

The photo showed dozens of naked and emaciated corpses piled in a heap, and that was all. I remember being viscerally shocked and frightened by what I saw, and I immediately realized that the dead people who appeared in the photo were the victims of human monsters.

I thought about that photo for weeks, and I finally comforted myself with the childish conviction that death camps would never come to America—that Americans could never commit such savage acts.

I was naïve of course. As I grew older, I realized there are plenty of Americans who will do anything they are directed to do—no matter how much pain they inflict on other human beings.

The people who operated the Nazi death camps were, after all, ordinary people. They probably read their morning newspapers over breakfast and played with their children after work in the evenings.

They labored for the Nazi death machine for a variety of mundane reasons—maybe they just needed a paycheck.

And this brings me to the lawyers who work for Educational Credit Management Corporation (ECMC), perhaps the federal government's most ruthless debt collector against student-loan borrowers.[1] ECMC's attorneys have gone into bankruptcy court time after time to oppose debt relief for distressed student-loan debtors. In the *Roth* case, for example, ECMC's legal counsel opposed bankruptcy relief for Janet Roth, an elderly debtor with chronic health problems who was living on less than $800 a month. ECMC harried Ms. Roth all the way to the Ninth Circuit's Bankruptcy Appellate Panel.[2]

In a letter dated July 7, 2015, Lynn Mahaffie, a DOE bureaucrat, issued a letter advising creditors like ECMC not to oppose bankruptcy relief for student debtors if the cost of fighting a bankruptcy discharge did not make the effort worthwhile.[3]

But that letter was just bullshit. The DOE and its loan collectors almost always oppose bankruptcy relief for student-loan debtors—whether or not it is cost effective to do so. For example, in *Acosta-Conniff v. Educational Credit Management Corporation*, an Alabama bankruptcy judge discharged Alexandra Acosta-Conniff's student-loan debt.[4] Conniff was a single mother of two children working as

---

1 Natalie Kitroeff, "Loan Monitor Is Accused of Ruthless Tactics on Student Debt," *New York Times*, January 1, 2014, accessed August 4, 2017, http://www.nytimes.com/2014/01/02/us/loan-monitor-is-accused-of-ruthless-tactics-on-student-debt.html?_r=0.

2 Roth v. Educational Credit Management Corporation, 490 B. R. 908 (B.A.P. 9th Cir. 2013).

3 Letter from Lynn Mahaffie, Deputy Assistant Secretary for Policy, Planning and Innovation, "Undue Hardship Discharge of Title IV Loans in Bankruptcy Adversary Proceedings," DCL ID: Gen-15-13, July 7, 2017, accessed August 3, 2017, https://ifap.ed.gov/dpcletters/attachments/GEN1513.pdf.

4 Acosta-Conniff v. ECMC (Educational Credit Management Corporation), 536 B.R. 326 (Bankr. M.D. Ala. 2015), *rev'd*, 550 B.R. 557 (M.D. Ala. 2016), *vacated*

a schoolteacher, and the court reasoned quite sensibly that Conniff would not be able to pay off her student loans.

ECMC dispatched six attorneys to appeal the bankruptcy court's decision: David Edwin Rains, Kristofer David Sodergren, Rachel Lavender Webber, Robert Allen Morgan, Margaret Hammond Manuel, and David Chip Schwartz. Six attorneys—and Conniff didn't even have a lawyer!

Not surprisingly, ECMC won its appeal before an Alabama federal district court.[5] Six lawyers against a single mother of two who couldn't afford an attorney was hardly a fair fight.

But then Conniff obtained an attorney and appealed the district court's unfavorable ruling to the Eleventh Circuit Court of Appeals, where she obtained a partial victory.[6] ECMC had a platoon of lawyers to represent it before the Eleventh Circuit, and who knows how much that cost?

But ECMC apparently doesn't care how much the appeal will cost, and the DOE obviously doesn't care either. Otherwise, it would direct its loan collectors not to harass insolvent student-loan debtors in the bankruptcy courts.

Now, I am not comparing ECMC's lawyers to Nazi death-camp workers. Being a debt collector's attorney is not intrinsically evil, and any misery inflicted on a student-loan debtor in a bankruptcy court is trivial compared to the horrors of Auschwitz. I feel sure ECMC's lawyers are all decent people.

---

and remanded, No. 16-12884, 2017 U.S. App. LEXIS 6746 (11th Cir. April 19, 2017) (unpublished decision).

5 Educational Credit Management Corporation v. Acosta-Conniff, 550 B.R. 557 (M.D. Ala. 2016), *vacated and remanded*, No. 16-12884, 2017 U.S. App. LEXIS 6746 (11th Cir. April 19, 2017) (unpublished decision).

6 Acosta-Conniff v. Educational Credit Management Corporation, No. 16-12884, 2017 U.S. App. LEXIS 6746 (11th Cir. April 19, 2017) (unpublished decision).

Nevertheless, I personally could not sleep at night if I were representing ECMC in the bankruptcy courts against people like Janet Roth or Alexandra Acosta-Conniff. I would ask myself whether I were serving the interests of justice by helping ECMC deprive honest but unfortunate college-loan borrowers of a fresh start in life.

But I don't imagine ECMC's attorneys ask themselves that question. And I doubt whether they have trouble sleeping at night. After all, the lawyers have their own student loans to pay off, and everyone has to make a living.

Parent PLUS Loans Can Be a Nightmare:
Teach Your Children Well

• • •

Teach your children well,
Their father's hell did slowly go by.

—GRAHAM NASH
"TEACH THE CHILDREN WELL"

MORE THAN THREE MILLION PARENTS have taken out student loans for their children's college educations. Eleven percent are in default, and another 180,000 are delinquent in their payments.

Congress created the Parent PLUS program in 1980, which allows parents to obtain student loans to supplement the loans their children take out to finance their college studies. As Josh Mitchell reported in the *Wall Street Journal* recently, outstanding indebtedness on Parent PLUS loans now tops $77 billion.[1]

The government issues Parent PLUS loans with little regard for whether the parents can pay them back. Many parents who take out Parent PLUS loans have subprime credit scores, which means they

---

1 Josh Mitchell, "The U.S. Makes It Easy for Parents to Get College Loans—Repaying Them Is Another Story," *Wall Street Journal*, April 24, 2017, accessed August 4, 2017, https://www.wsj.com/articles/the-u-s-makes-it-easy-for-parents-to-get-college-loansrepaying-them-is-another-story-1493047388.

run a high risk of default. As Mitchell pointed out, the Parent PLUS default rate is higher than the home-mortgage default rate during the 2008 housing crisis.

Without question, Parent PLUS loans are being issued recklessly. "This credit is being extended on terms that specifically, willfully ignore their ability to repay," a spokesperson for Harvard Law School's Legal Services Center charged. "You can't avoid that we're targeting high-cost, high-dollar-amount loans to people who we know can't afford them."

To its credit, the Obama administration recognized that lending standards for Parent PLUS loans were too lax. In 2011, the DOE introduced modest underwriting rules to prevent parents with low credit ratings from taking out Parent PLUS loans.

But the higher-education industry protested, arguing that tighter underwriting standards for Parent PLUS loans would reduce college access for low-income and minority students. In response to this pressure, the DOE withdrew the new rules.

Obviously, people who are taking out student loans for their children are older; two-thirds of Parent PLUS borrowers are between the ages of fifty and sixty-four. Many of them have student loans of their own. Some parents took out Parent PLUS loans expecting their children to get good jobs and take over the loan payments. But sometimes that doesn't happen, and the parents find themselves responsible for paying off loans they can't afford to repay.

Parents who default on Parent PLUS loans risk having their income-tax refunds seized and their Social Security checks garnished. And bankruptcy is rarely an option. Parents who default on their children's student loans will find it difficult to discharge those loans in bankruptcy even if they are unemployed or in ill health.

In an NPR podcast, Michelle Singletary, a finance columnist, pointed out that many parents take out Parent PLUS loans to help their children attend expensive colleges their families can't afford. It is difficult, Singletary acknowledged, for parents to tell their children that a particular elite college is simply out of financial reach.

The child might say, "But this is my dream college." If that happens, Singletary advised, the parent must have the wisdom and fortitude to say, "Honey, you need to find another dream."[2]

Or, as songwriter Graham Nash might put it, "teach your children well" regarding their college choices because if you borrow money for your child to go to college and can't pay it back, you will enter financial hell, a hell that will go by slowly.

2 Tom Ashbrook, "Parents on the Hook for Student Loans," *NPR Onpoint* (podcast), April 26, 2017, http://www.wbur.org/onpoint/2017/04/26/parents-student-loans.

Parents Who Take Out PLUS Student Loans to Pay for Their Children's College Educations: Don't Be Fools

• • •

Most country-and-western songs are about regret: I'm sorry I cheated on my wife, I regret mouthing off to a biker in the honky-tonk, or I wish I hadn't shot a man in Reno.

I don't know of any country-and-western song about student loans, but there should be. A recent survey reported that about 50 percent of student-loan debtors regretted how much they borrowed to go to college. More than a third said they would not have gone to college had they realized what it would cost them.[1]

But the people who are really, really sorry are the parents who took out loans to pay for their children's college educations. If they cosigne a private loan for a child, they are on the hook for it, even if their child dies. And parents will find it is virtually impossible to discharge a cosigned student loan in bankruptcy, whether it is a private loan or a federally subsidized loan.

In fact, I say this unequivocally: Parents should never borrow money to pay for their child's college education.

Yet our federal government peddles Parent PLUS loans—student loans taken out by parents—as a good way to help finance a

---

1 Citizens Bank, "Millennial College Graduates with Student Loans Now Spending Nearly One-Fifth of Their Annual Salaries on Student Loan Repayments," April 7, 2016, accessed August 4, 2017, http://investor.citizensbank.com/about-us/newsroom/latest-news/2016/2016-04-07-140336028.aspx.

child's college costs. The DOE recently posted a blog telling parents that "PLUS loans are an excellent option if you need money to pay your child's educational expenses," although it cautions that parents need to make sure they understand the loan terms before they take out a PLUS loan.[2]

And what are those terms? The DOE's blog posting says that the current interest rate is 6.31 percent and that monthly repayment begins immediately. Monthly PLUS loan payments are not postponed while the child is still in college.

The DOE then summarizes various PLUS loan repayment plans, including an income-contingent plan (ICR) that allows parents to pay 20 percent of their discretionary income for twenty-five years.

Of course, it is madness for parents to pay a fifth of their discretionary income for twenty-five years in order for a child to go to college. There are lots of college options that don't require that kind of sacrifice.

The DOE assures parents that any unpaid balance on their PLUS loan will be forgiven after twenty-five years. But note that the DOE doesn't tell parents that they could face a big tax bill for the amount of the loan that is forgiven.

And the DOE doesn't warn parents that they will find it almost impossible to discharge a PLUS loan in bankruptcy should they run into financial trouble due to illness, job loss, or some other financial calamity.

The DOE ends its deceptive blog on this cheery note: "Yes, there's lots to consider when it comes to taking out a Direct PLUS loan, but there are many benefits to getting one if you need help paying your child's education."[3]

---

2 Lisa Rhodes, "PLUS Loan Basics for Parents," *Homeroom* (blog), August 8, 2016, accessed August 3, 2017, https://blog.ed.gov/2016/08/plus-loan-basics-parents/.
3 Ibid.

In fact, there's *nothing* to consider. If your children can't finance their college educations without you going into debt, then they need to develop other plans.

My guess is that a lot of parents take out PLUS loans to help their kids go to fancy East Coast private schools, which is foolish. If your children cannot afford to go to Harvard or Dartmouth or Amherst without putting you into debt, then they need to enroll at nearby public universities and take part-time jobs at McDonald's.

Trust me. You and your children will be better off if you avoid all college options that force Mom and Pop to go into debt. Johnny Cash was sorry he shot that guy in Reno, but he was not any sorrier than you will be if you take out a loan to send your child to college.

If You Had to Enroll in a Twenty-Five-Year Income-Based Repayment Plan to Pay for Your College Education, You Attended the Wrong College

• • •

IN HIS 2012 BOOK ENTITLED *Don't Go to Law School (Unless)*, Paul Campos made a statement that startled me by its intense clarity. "The truth is," Campos wrote, "that people who are likely to end up in [income-based repayment plans] if they go to law school should not go at all."[1]

And of course, Campos is right. But isn't the same observation true about undergraduate education as well? A person who must enter a twenty-five-year IBRP to pay for a college degree either enrolled in the wrong college or chose the wrong academic major—and probably both.

For example, Ron Lieber of the *New York Times* wrote a story in 2010 that featured Cortney Munna, who borrowed almost $100,000 to get an interdisciplinary degree in religious and women's studies at New York University, one of the most expensive universities in the world. At the time of Lieber's story, Munna was working for a photographer for twenty-two dollars an hour and enrolled in night school, "which allow[ed] her to defer her loan payments."[2]

---

1 Paul Campos, *Don't Go To Law School (Unless)*, (Lexington, KY: CreateSpace Independent Publishing Platform, 2012), 48.

2 Ron Lieber, "Placing the Blame as Students Are Buried in Debt," *New York Times*, May 28, 2010, accessed August 3, 2017, http://www.nytimes.com/2010/05/29/your-money/student-loans/29money.html.

As Lieber pointed out, going back to college simply to postpone student-loan payments on the degree one already has is not a good long-term option because interest continues to accrue on the debt.

I wonder how Ms. Munna is doing today. I think the chances are very good that she is in a twenty-five-year IBRP.

Campos said in his book that "there's a good argument to be made that law schools [that] promote IBR [income-based repayment plans] are participating in a fraud on the public."[3] Again, I think Campos is right.

Most people who enter into twenty-five-year IBRPs won't make payments large enough to cover accruing interest and also pay down the principal on their loans. In other words, most people in IBRPs will see their loans negatively amortize. This means the taxpayer will be left holding the bag when the loan's repayment term ends and the unpaid portion of the loan is forgiven.

To return to Ms. Munna's story, shouldn't New York University bear some responsibility for allowing her to borrow so much money for a degree that was not likely to lead to a job that would allow her to pay back the debt?

Of course, universities are not in the habit of admitting that some of their degree programs are overpriced. But maybe it is a habit they should acquire. How many private universities could look their students in the eye and say their degrees in women's studies, religious studies, sociology, urban studies, and so forth are worth going $100,000 into debt? Not many.

---

3 Paul Campos, *Don't Go To Law School (Unless)*, (Lexington, KY: CreateSpace Independent Publishing Platform, 2012), 50.

Income-Driven Repayment Plans for Managing Crushing Levels of Student-Loan Debt: Financial Suicide

• • •

BY THE END OF HIS first term in office, President Obama knew the federal student-loan program was out of control. Default rates were up, and millions of student borrowers had put their loans into forbearance or deferment because they were unable to make their monthly payments. Then in 2013, early in Obama's second term, the Consumer Financial Protection Bureau issued a comprehensive report titled *A Closer Look at the Trillion* that sketched out the magnitude of the crisis.[1]

What to do? President Obama chose to promote IDRs to give borrowers short-term relief from oppressive monthly loan payments. Obama's DOE rolled out two generous IDRs: the PAYE program, which was announced in 2012, and REPAYE, introduced in 2016.

PAYE and REPAYE both require borrowers to make monthly payments equal to 10 percent of their discretionary income for twenty years: 240 payments in all. Borrowers who make regular payments but do not pay off their loans by the end of the repayment period will have their loans forgiven, but the cancelled debt is taxable to them as income.

---

1 Rohit Chopra, "A Closer Look at the Trillion," *Consumer Financial Protection Bureau* (blog), August 5, 2013, https://www.consumerfinance.gov/about-us/blog/a-closer-look-at-the-trillion/.

The higher-education industry loves PAYE and REPAYE, and what's not to like? Neither plan requires colleges and universities to keep their costs in line or operate more efficiently. Students will continue borrowing more and more money to pay exorbitant tuition prices, but monthly payments will be manageable because they will be spread out over twenty years rather than ten.

But most people enrolling in PAYE or REPAYE are signing their own financial death warrants. By shifting to long-term IDRs, they become indentured servants to the government, paying percentages of their incomes for the majority of their working lives.

And, as illustrated in *Murray v. Educational Credit Management Corporation* in 2016, an ongoing bankruptcy action, a lot of people who sign up for IDRs will be stone broke on the date they make their final payment.[2] In that case, a Kansas bankruptcy judge granted a partial discharge of student-loan debt to Alan and Catherine Murray. The Murrays borrowed $77,000 to get bachelor's and master's degrees, and they paid back 70 percent of what they borrowed.

Unfortunately, the Murrays were unable to make their monthly payments for a time, and they put their loans into deferment. Interest accrued over the years, and by the time they filed for bankruptcy, their student-loan indebtedness had grown to $311,000—four times what they had borrowed.

A bankruptcy judge concluded that the Murrays had handled their loans in good faith but would never pay back their enormous debt—debt that was growing at the rate of $2,000 a month due to accruing interest. Thus, the judge discharged the interest on their debt, requiring them only to pay back the original amount they borrowed.

ECMC, the Murrays' student-loan creditor, argued unsuccessfully that the Murrays should be placed in a twenty- or twenty-five-year

---

2 Murray v. Educational Credit Management Corporation, 563 B.R. 52 (Bankr. D. Kan. 2016).

IDR. The bankruptcy judge rejected ECMC's demand, pointing out that the Murrays would never pay back the amount they owed and would be faced with a huge tax bill twenty years later when their loan balance would be forgiven.

ECMC appealed, arguing that the bankruptcy judge erred when he took tax consequences into account when he granted the Murrays a partial discharge of their student loans. Tax consequences are speculative, ECMC insisted, and in any event, the Murrays would almost certainly be insolvent at the end of the twenty-year repayment term, and therefore, they would not have to pay taxes on the forgiven loan balance.

What an astonishing admission! ECMC basically conceded that the Murrays would be broke at the end of a twenty-year repayment plan, when they would be in their late sixties.

So, if you are a struggling student-loan borrower who is considering an IDR, the *Murray* case is a cautionary tale. If you elect this option, you almost certainly will never pay off your student loans because your monthly payments won't cover accumulating interest.

Thus, at the end of your repayment period—twenty or twenty-five years from now—one of two things will happen. Either you will be faced with a huge tax bill because the amount of your forgiven loan is considered income by the IRS, or—as ECMC disarmingly admitted in the *Murray* case—you will be broke.

Liz Kelly, a Schoolteacher, Owes $410,000 in Student Loans—Most of It Accumulated Interest. Will She Ever Pay It Back?

● ● ●

LIZ KELLY, A FORTY-EIGHT-YEAR-OLD SCHOOLTEACHER, owes the federal government $410,000 in student loans, which she will almost certainly never pay back. How did that happen?

COMPOUND INTEREST

As a *New York Times* story reported, Kelly didn't borrow $410,000 to finance her studies. She actually borrowed less than $150,000. Two-thirds of her total debt is accumulated interest.[1]

Over the years, Kelly took out student loans to pay for her undergraduate education and graduate studies as well as her childcare and living expenses. She also borrowed money to get a law degree, which she did not complete, and a PhD from Texas A&M, which she also did not complete.

Her graduate studies enabled her to postpone making payments on her loans, but she continued borrowing more money; and the interest on her loans continued to accrue. Some of her loans accrued

---

1 Kevin Carey, "Lend With A Smile: Collect With A Fist," *New York Times*, November 27, 2015, accessed August 6, 2017, https://www.nytimes.com/2015/11/29/upshot/student-debt-in-america-lend-with-a-smile-collect-with-a-fist.html?_r=0.

interest at 8.25 percent—a pretty high interest rate. When her total indebtedness reached $260,000, she consolidated her student loans at 7 percent interest, which is still pretty high.[2]

Over a period of twenty-five years, Kelly received a series of forbearances or deferments, and she allegedly never made a single payment on her loans over that time period.[3] Thus, it is easy to understand how the total amount of her indebtedness tripled over the amount she borrowed. In fact, as the *New York Times* article pointed out, the annual cost of interest on her unpaid student loans is now larger than the total amount she borrowed for her under-graduate education.

Back in the old days, when people received interest on their sav-ings, most people understood the principle of compound interest. People knew, for example, that money saved at 7 percent interest doubled in ten years and that money saved at 10 percent interest doubled in seven years.

But no one gets interest on their savings any more, and per-haps that explains why many student-loan borrowers don't realize that their total indebtedness grows every year their loans are in deferment. Liz Kelly apparently didn't understand this. The *Times* reported that she was shocked to learn that she owed $410,000.

No Cap on Student Loans

Although Kelly did not make a single payment on her student loans over a 25-year span, the federal government continued to loan her money. In fact, in 2011, she borrowed about $7,500 to pursue a PhD in education, even though her total indebtedness at that time was more than a third of a million dollars, and she had made no loan payments.

---

2 Ibid.
3 Ibid.

As the *Times* writer succinctly observed,

> A private sector lender approached by a potential borrower
> with no assets, a modest income, and $350,000 in debt who
> had never made a payment on that loan in over twenty years
> would not, presumably, lend that person an addition $7,800.
> But that is exactly what the federal government did for Ms.
> Kelly. Legally it could do nothing else.[4]

Obviously, a federal student-loan system that works this way is dysfunctional, irrational, and unsustainable. The feds should have shut off the student-loan spigot long before Kelly borrowed money to get a PhD.

THE CHARADE OF INCOME-BASED REPAYMENT PLANS

If Kelly had accumulated $410,000 in consumer debt or on a home mortgage, she could discharge the debt in bankruptcy. But discharging a student loan in bankruptcy is very hard to do. Indeed, the Bankruptcy Code specifically provides that student loans cannot be discharged in bankruptcy unless the debtor can show that the student-loan obligation creates an "undue hardship," a very difficult standard to meet.[5]

Kelly's only reasonable escape from her predicament is to enroll in the federal government's loan forgiveness program, which would allow her to make payments based on a percentage of her income for a period of ten years, so long as she works in an approved public-service job. As a schoolteacher, she should easily qualify for this program.

---

4 Ibid.
5 11 U.S.C. §523(a)(8).

But as Kelly herself pointed out, her monthly loan payments under such a plan would not even cover accumulating interest on the $410,000 she owes. At the end of her ten-year repayment program, her total indebtedness would be larger than it is now—easily a half million dollars. That amount would be forgiven, leaving the taxpayers on the hook.

In fact, Kelly's situation is a perfect illustration for the argument that income-driven repayment plans (IDRs) are not a solution to the student-loan crisis. Most people who participate in them—more than 5 million people—will not pay down the principal on their loans. IDRs are really just a penance for borrowing too much money—say one Our Father and three Hail Marys, and go and sin no more.

Conclusion

The *Times* story on Liz Kelly concluded with the observation that Kelly's story is unusual, but that's not really true. As the *Times* itself observed in a 2015 editorial, 10 million people have either defaulted on their loans or are in delinquency.[6] The Consumer Financial Protection Bureau reported in 2013 that nearly 9 million people were not making payments on their student loans because they had obtained a forbearance or a deferment.[7] And more than 5 million people are in IDRs.[8]

---

6 "Why Student Debtors Go Unrescued," *New York Times*, October 7, 2015, accessed, August 5, 2017, https://www.nytimes.com/2015/10/07/opinion/why-student-debtors-go-unrescued.html.

7 Rohit Chopra, "A Closer Look at the Trillion," *Consumer Financial Protection Bureau* (blog), August 5, 2013, https://www.consumerfinance.gov/about-us/blog/a-closer-look-at-the-trillion/.

8 Danielle Douglas-Gabriel, "It's going to cost taxpayers $108 billion to help student loan borrowers," *Washington Post*, November 30, 2016, accessed August 6, 2017.

Thus, at least 23 million people have loans in the repayment phase and are not making standard loan payments. So what should we do?

1. The federal government should not loan people more money if they are not making payments on the money they already borrowed. No one did Liz Kelly any favors by loaning her an additional $7,500 when she had already accumulated indebtedness of $350,000 and didn't have a prayer of ever paying it back.
2. There needs to be some cap on the amount of money people can borrow from the federal student-loan program. I'm not prepared to say what the cap should be, but surely it is bad public policy to lend money so that people can accumulate multiple degrees that do not further their financial prospects.
3. We've got to face the fact that IDRs are not a solution to the student-loan crisis. Surely it is pointless to put Kelly on a long-term IDR that won't even pay the interest on her debt.

As unpalatable as it is for politicians and the higher-education community to admit, bankruptcy is the only humane option for people like Liz Kelly. Did she make some mistakes in managing her financial affairs? Yes. But the federal government and several universities allowed her to make those mistakes, and the universities received the benefit of Kelly's tuition money.

No, we need to face this plain and simple fact: Kelly will never pay off that $410,000. And putting her in an IDR is nothing more than a strategy to avoid facing reality, which is this: the federal student-loan program is out of control.

Kelly v. Sallie Mae and Educational Credit Management Corporation: Fees, Interest, and Penalties Are Dragging Down Student-Loan Debtors

• • •

SOME POLICY EXPERTS ARGUE THAT there is no crisis in the student-loan program. Most students borrow only modest amounts of money, the experts say. The people who owe more than $100,000 are just a tiny fraction of the 43 million student-loan borrowers.

But this argument fails to take into account interest, penalties, and fees that borrowers accumulate if they run into financial trouble and can't make their loan payments. Some distressed borrowers obtain economic-hardship deferments or forbearances that excuse them from making payments. But the fees and interest amounts that accrue over time can double, triple, or even quadruple the sizes of their loan balances. When that happens, they are doomed.

And here's a case that illustrates my point: *Kelly v. Sallie Mae, Inc.*[1] Laura Kelly borrowed about $24,000 to pay for her undergraduate degree in political science at Seattle University. She made payments for several years, but she ran into financial trouble and stopped making payments. In 2008, she filed for bankruptcy.[2]

---

1 Educational Credit Management v. Kelly, No. C11–1263RSL, 2012 WL 1378725 (W.D. Wash. April 20, 2012), *rev'd*, Kelly v. Sallie Mae, Inc., 594 F. App'x. 413 (9th Cir. 2015) (unpublished decision).
2 Ibid., *1.

By the time Kelly entered bankruptcy, her debt had more than *quadrupled* to $105,000 due to collection fees and accumulated interest.[3] She filed an adversary proceeding to clear this debt, and a bankruptcy court gave her a partial discharge. The court concluded that Kelly was unable to pay off her loans, that her financial situation was not likely to improve soon, and that she had acted in good faith in the way she had handled her indebtedness.

Educational Credit Management Corporation, perhaps the federal government's most aggressive debt collector, appealed the bankruptcy court's decision, and a federal district court reversed the lower court's ruling.[4] The district court upheld the lower court's conclusion that Kelly could not pay back the hundred grand and still maintain a minimal standard of living. And it upheld the conclusion that Kelly's financial situation would not improve soon.

But the district court reversed the bankruptcy court's ruling that Kelly had acted in good faith. The district court thought Kelly should have explored alternative payment plans, including a public-service loan-payment program. And it also believed she could cut her expenses and make some sort of loan payment. "In short," the district court ruled, "Ms. Kelly made no effort, much less good faith effort, to repay her loans."[5]

Proceeding without a lawyer, Kelly appealed the district court's opinion to the next level: the Ninth Circuit Court of Appeals. The Ninth Circuit, which was considerably more compassionate than the district court, reversed the district court's decision and reinstated the bankruptcy court's partial discharge. This is what the Ninth Circuit said:

---

3 Ibid.
4 Ibid.
5 Ibid., *3.

The bankruptcy court justified its conclusion that Kelly had acted in good faith with reference to its findings that, among other things, Kelly had maximized her income, had incurred only marginally excessive expenses, paid thousands of dollars toward her student debt over an eight year period before filing for bankruptcy, and at least minimally investigated payment alternatives such as debt consolidation, deferment, and a federal loan repayment program...Moreover, though Kelly did not pursue loan repayment options, the bankruptcy court did not clearly err in its conclusion that Kelly had a good-faith belief that she was ineligible for the program, and that applying for the program would have been futile since she could not afford the payments after consolidation.[6]

The Ninth Circuit's Kelly decision is significant for three reasons:

1. Kelly successfully fought Sallie Mae and ECMC, two of the federal government's most sophisticated and relentless debt collectors, without a lawyer all the way to the Ninth Circuit. But consider how long the process took. Kelly filed for bankruptcy in 2008, and the Ninth Circuit didn't issue its opinion until 2015. Most debtors would not have the stamina for a seven-year court fight, which is what ECMC and Sallie Mae were probably counting on. Thus, Kelly should be saluted as a hero for fighting ECMC and Sallie Mae for so long.
2. The *Kelly* decision is one of a string of recent federal appellate court decisions that ruled in favor of student-loan debtors. *Kelly* is not as significant as the Ninth Circuit Bankruptcy Appellate Panel's *Roth* decision or the Seventh Circuit's

---

6 Kelly v. Sallie Mae, Inc., 594 F. App'x. 413, 414 (9th Cir. 2015) (unpublished decision).

Krieger decision.[7] Nevertheless, by upholding the bankruptcy court's decision to grant Kelly some relief, the Ninth Circuit has signaled that it will support compassionate bankruptcy courts that rule in favor of student-loan debtors if those rulings are grounded in solid fact findings.

3. Most importantly, *Kelly v. Sallie Mae and Educational Credit Management Corporation* dramatically demonstrates how penalties, accumulated interest amounts, and collection fees can turn a manageable debt into a nightmare. Kelly only borrowed $24,000 to pay for her college education. By the time she arrived in bankruptcy court, the debt had quadrupled in spite of the fact that she had made loan payments for eight years.

Our government has designed a student-loan program that is totally insane. For many students, it is the fees, penalties, and accumulated interest amounts that are sinking them—not the amounts of the original debts.

---

7 Roth v. Educational Credit Management Corporation, 409 B. R. 908 (B.A.P. 9th Cir. 2013); Krieger v. Educational Credit Management Corporation, 713 F.3d 882 (7th Cir. 2013).

How Many College Graduates Have Jobs that Don't Require a College Degree? You Might Be Surprised

• • •

THE FEDERAL RESERVE BANK OF New York recently released an analysis of labor-market conditions for college graduates.[1] Here is a summary of what it found:

* In 2015, almost 45 percent of recent college graduates (graduates aged twenty-two through twenty-seven) were working in jobs that *did not* require a college degree.
* Around 35 percent of *all* graduates (graduates aged twenty-two through sixty-five) were holding down jobs that didn't require a college education.
* Wages for recent college graduates remained relatively flat from 1990 to 2015.

So what do these numbers mean for young Americans?

COLLEGE IS NOT A GOOD BET FOR EVERYONE

First, although the college industry and its advocates like to remind us that people who graduate from college make more money over

---

1 Federal Reserve Bank of New York, *The Labor Market for Recent College Graduates*, accessed August 5, 2017, https://www.newyorkfed.org/research/college-labor-market/index.html.

their lifetimes than people who only have high-school diplomas, going to college is not a good bet for everyone.

As the New York Fed has shown us, darn near half of recent college graduates are working in jobs they could have gotten without going to college. Of course, many recent graduates will eventually find jobs that require college degrees. But even among the college-educated population as a whole, about one-third of college graduates are working in jobs that do not require a college education.

The Payoff for Getting a College Degree Is Not as Good as It Once Was

Second, wages for college graduates have remained about the same for the past twenty-five years—about $45,000 in constant 2015 dollars. But the cost of going to college has tripled over the last quarter of a century. That's why about two thirds of college graduates leave school with college-loan debt.

Thus, you may still need to go to college to earn a decent income, but a portion of that income is going to go to servicing student loans. In other words, recent college graduates are not as well off financially as their counterparts were in 1990 because a majority of them are graduating with a significant amount of debt.

The Case for a Free College Education Gets Stronger and Stronger

People laughed at Bernie Sanders during the 2016 presidential campaign when he argued for a free college education from a public college for anyone who wants one. But Bernie's plan would actually cost less than the current federal loan program, because millions of people aren't paying off their loans.

Certainly offering a free college education makes more sense than loaning billions of dollars to people to get college degrees they don't need for the jobs they have, especially when a lot of those dollars will never be paid back.

Know When to Fold 'Em: Dropping Out of Graduate School May Make More Economic Sense than Continuing in a Program that Will Not Pay Off

• • •

GRADUATE SCHOOL HAS GOTTEN INCREDIBLY expensive, and it is increasingly obvious that borrowing money to obtain a graduate degree is not always a good financial bet. In fact, in *Don't Go to Law School (Unless)*, law professor Paul Campos argued that law students who borrow a lot of money to attend a second- or third-tier law school and don't excel academically in their first year should consider quitting law school rather than borrowing more money to get a degree that probably won't lead to a good job.[1]

It is true that people who quit law school lose their entire investments. They've taken out loans to pay for degrees they will never get. And many people will be tempted to borrow more money in order to pay for two more years of study that will lead to a JD degree. But Campos argues that this is the wrong choice for many people— particularly for people who got mediocre grades during their first years at mediocre law schools.

Campos's advice to law students applies to all kinds of graduate programs. People who borrow money to get PhDs in sociology, medieval history, or English from second-tier graduate schools may

---

1 Paul Campos, *Don't Go to Law School (Unless)*, (Lexington, KY: CreateSpace Independent Publishing Platform, 2012), 84-90.

realize early in their studies that getting well-paying jobs in their chosen fields is highly unlikely. For these people, it may make financial sense to drop out of graduate school rather than continue to borrow more money.

But graduate students who quit their degree programs and then seek to discharge their student loans in bankruptcy will inevitably face opposition from student-loan creditors who will argue that the dropouts failed to make a good-faith effort to maximize their incomes and thus should be denied bankruptcy relief.

Fortunately, the Eighth Circuit Court of Appeals, in the case of *Shaffer v. US Department of Education*, understood the economic rationale behind some people's decisions to drop out of graduate school.[2] The case involved Susan Shaffer, a woman with significant mental health problems who borrowed $204,000 for her postsecondary studies, including money she borrowed to pursue a graduate degree at Palmer College of Chiropractic Medicine.

A bankruptcy judge discharged all of Shaffer's loans, but the Iowa Student Loan Liquidity Corporation, one of her creditors, appealed the decision. Iowa Student Loan argued that Shaffer's low income (she was living on about $1,700 a month) was self-imposed because she had dropped out of her chiropractic program. According to Iowa Student Loan, Shaffer should have borrowed more money in order to stay in school and get her chiropractic degree, which would have led to a high-paying job that would have allowed her to pay off her student loans.

But a panel of Eighth Circuit judges emphatically rejected that argument, saying there was no support for Iowa Student Loan's position in the trial court record. On the other hand, the appellate court pointed out that the bankruptcy court had heard Shaffer's explanation for why she had dropped out of the chiropractic program and had found her testimony credible.

---

2 Shaffer v. US Department of Education, 481 B. R. 15 (8th Cir. 2012).

As the Eighth Circuit colloquially put the matter, Iowa Student Loan's contention that Shaffer should have stayed in graduate school were "contrary to the sage advice of both Will Rogers, who said, 'When you find yourself in a hole, stop digging,' and Kenny Rogers, who sang, 'You got to know...when to fold 'em.'"[3]

Apparently, the bankruptcy court had concluded that Shaffer's mental health challenges made her unfit for some higher-paying jobs, presumably including a job in the field of chiropractic medicine. As the Eight Circuit observed, "The bankruptcy court determined that [the debtor] could endure only work that was essentially ministerial and that she suffered from the stress of increased responsibility due to a lack of self-confidence. While there was no evidence that the debtor was clinically disabled or maladjusted, the bankruptcy court expressly found that [the debtor] was not fit for the higher responsibility and higher paying positions she tried and then left."

Interestingly, Shaffer presented no expert witnesses to buttress her testimony about her mental-health challenges. Iowa Student Loan argued that the bankruptcy court had engaged in impermissible speculation when it concluded that Shaffer's mental health issues were an obstacle to getting a high-paying job.

But the Eighth Circuit disagreed. "The bankruptcy court heard Debtor's testimony, judged her credibility, and accepted her description of her mental health issues and their effect on her ability to maintain employment...Consequently, we cannot say the bankruptcy court's findings were clearly erroneous."

The *Shaffer* decision is a good decision for any student-loan debtor in bankruptcy who borrowed money to go to graduate school and then dropped out. The court accepted Shaffer's explanation for why it did not make economic sense for her to continue her chiropractic studies, and the court did not require Shaffer to hire an expert witness to corroborate her testimony.

---

3 Ibid.

Department of Education Executives Pay Themselves Cash Bonuses While the Federal Student-Loan Program Goes to Hell

• • •

AT LAST, THE SECRET IS out. The federal student-loan program is out of control, and millions of borrowers cannot pay back their loans. As the *New York Times* pointed out in a recent editorial, student debtors are defaulting at an average rate of three thousand a day—more than a million people went into default last year alone.[1]

But the DOE hacks who oversee the student-loan program have been paying themselves performance bonuses. James Runcie, chief operating officer for the DOE's student-loan program, received $433,000 in bonuses, and then he resigned rather than testify before the House Oversight Committee about what the heck was going on in the loan program he supervised.

And Runcie was not the only DOE executive to get bonuses. The National Association of Student Financial Aid Administrators (NASFAA) released a report in May 2017 that provides some useful information about how the DOE's bonus program works.[2]

---

1 "The Wrong Move on Student Loans," *New York Times,* April 6, 2017, accessed August 3 2017, https://www.nytimes.com/2017/04/06/opinion/the-wrong-move-on-student-loans.html?_r=0.

2 National Association of Student Financial Aid Administrators, *Improving Oversight and Transparency at the US Department of Education's Financial Aid:*

As the NASFAA report explains, the Federal Student Aid Office (FSA) set performance goals for the organization and then basically assessed itself with regard to whether the office met those goals. According to NASFAA, "self-assessments are a common way to begin performance evaluations, but they are usually signed off on by a person or board with oversight responsibility."[3] The FSA, however, let its own evaluations stand "without pushback, oversight, or accountability, which often easily allows the organization to excuse away failure to meet goals and targets."[4]

FSA's self-assessment program permitted senior executives to get bonuses if they excelled at their work. The program identified three categories of performance: exceptional, high results, or results achieved. Note that there was no category for poor performance.

Senior people who scored exceptional or high results were eligible for bonuses, and not surprisingly, performance scores got higher and higher as the years went by. In FY 2011, "66 percent of senior FSA leaders received an 'exceptional' or 'high results' performance rating that qualified them for bonuses. In FY 2015, 90 percent of senior administrators got those ratings.

Correspondingly, the percentage of eligible employees who only scored results achieved, making them ineligible for bonuses, decreased from 34 percent to only 10 percent between FY 2011 and FY 2015.

Bottom line is this: In FY 2015, 89.8 percent of FSA senior administrators ranked highly enough to get a cash bonus, and 89.8 percent of those administrators got cash bonuses. How big were the bonuses? I haven't seen a list showing bonus amounts and who

---

NASFAA's Recommendations (May 2017), https://www.nasfaa.org/uploads/documents/NASFAA_FSA_Report.pdf.

3 Ibid.

4 Ibid.

got them. The *Huffington Post* reported that at least one bonus was $75,000.[5]

No wonder Mr. Runcie resigned rather than answer questions before the House Oversight Committee. "I cannot in good conscience continue to be accountable as Chief Operating officer given the risk associated with the current environment at the Education Department," he is quoted as saying.[6]

What the hell does that mean? I have no idea. Mr. Runcie's bio shows that he received an MBA from Harvard Business School. Perhaps that is the kind of self-serving bureaucratic language one learns while pursuing an MBA at Harvard.

---

5 Shahien Nasiripour, "Education Department Secretly Reappoints Top Official Accused of Harming Students," *Huffington Post*, May 7, 2016, http://www.huffington-post.com/entry/education-dept-student-loans_us_5728fdebe4b0bc9cb044dc16.
6 Adam Harris, "Top Federal Student-Aid Official Resigns Over Congressional Testimony," *Chronicle of Higher Education*, May 24, 2017, accessed August 5, 2017, http://www.chronicle.com/blogs/ticker/top-federal-student-aid-official-resigns-over-congressional-testimony/118615.

Will the Student-Loan Crisis Bring Down the Economy? My Pessimistic View

● ● ●

MIKE KRIEGER RECENTLY POSTED A blog on *Liberty Blitzkrieg* in which he argued that two issues will dominate American politics in the coming years: healthcare and student loans. "Going forward," Krieger wrote, "I believe two issues will define the future of American politics: student loans and healthcare. Both these things… have crushed the youth and are prevent[ing] a generation from buying homes and starting families. The youth will eventually revolt, and student loans and healthcare will have to be dealt with in a very major way, not with tinkering around the edges."[1]

Krieger concluded his essay with this pessimistic observation: "Student loans and healthcare are both ticking time bombs and I see no real effort underway to tackle them at the macro level where they need to be addressed. Watch these two issues closely going forward, as I think fury at both will be the main driver behind the next populist wave."[2]

Krieger's dismal projection regarding student loans is supported by other commentators. Zack Friedman, writing in *Forbes.com*,

---

1 Mike Krieger, "Student Loans and Healthcare—Two Issues that Will Define American Politics Going Forward," *Liberty Blitzkrieg* (blog), May 4, 2017, accessed May 5, 2017, https://libertyblitzkrieg.com/2017/05/04/student-loans-and-healthcare-two-issues-that-will-define-american-politics-going-forward/.

2 Ibid.

reported that more than 44 million people are now burdened by $1.3 trillion in student loans.[3] And as the *New York Times* observed, about 10 million borrowers are either delinquent on their loans or in default.[4]

Moreover, a lot of this debt is carried by older Americans. A U.S. Government Accountability Office Report stated that 7 million Americans over age 50 are student loan debtors.[5] In fact, in 2015, 173,000 people had their Social Security checks garnished due to student loans that were in default.[6]

Borrowers carry debt levels of varying amounts, but the Fed reported that 2 million people owe $100,000 or more on student loans. Interestingly, people with small levels of debt are more likely to default than people who have high levels of indebtedness. In the 2009 cohort of student borrowers, 34 percent of people who owed $5,000 or less had defaulted within five years. Among people owing $100,000 or more, only 18 percent defaulted during this same period.[7]

And of course, default rates don't tell the full story. More than 5 million people have signed up for IDRs, and most are making payments so low they will never pay off their loans. Millions more have

---

3 Zack Friedman, "Student Loan Debt in 2017: a $1.3 Trillion Crisis," *Forbes. com*, February 21, 2017, accessed August 6, 2017, https://www.forbes.com/sites/zackfriedman/2017/02/21/student-loan-debt-statistics-2017/#5dd0898d5dab.

4 "Why Student Debtors Go Unrescued, *New York Times*, October 7, 2015, accessed August 6, 217, ://www.nytimes.com/2015/10/07/opinion/why-student-debtors-go-unrescued.html.

5 US Government Accountability Office, *Social Security Offsets: Improvement to Program Design Could Better Assist Older Student Borrowers with Obtaining Permitted Relief,* GAO-17-45 , 8-9, December 2016, http://www.gao.gov/assets/690/681722.pdf.

6 Ibid., 11.

7 Meta Brown et al., "Looking at Student Loan Defaults through a Larger Window," *Liberty Street Economics* (blog), February 19, 2015, accessed August 5, 2017, http://libertystreeteconomics.newyorkfed.org/2015/02/looking_at_student_loan_defaults_through_a_larger_window.html.

loans in deferment or forbearance, and those people aren't even making token loan payments. Meanwhile, interest is accruing on those loans, making it more difficult for borrowers to pay them off once they resume making payments.

Surely, this rising level of student-loan indebtedness has an impact on the American economy. According to the *New York Times*, student loans now constitute 11 percent of total household indebtedness—up from just 5 percent in 2008.[8] Obviously, Americans with burdensome levels of student-loan debt are finding it more difficult to buy homes, start families, save for retirement, or even purchase basic consumer items. No wonder sales at brick-and-mortar retail stores are down and the casual dining industry is on the skids.

So far, as Krieger pointed out, our government is tinkering around the edges of the student-loan crisis, making ineffective efforts to rein in the for-profit college industry and urging students to sign up for long-term income-driven repayment plans.

But this strategy is not working. According to the Government Accountability Office, about half the people who sign up for IDRs are kicked out for noncompliance with the plans' terms. The for-profit colleges, beaten back a bit by reform efforts during President Obama's administration, have come roaring back during the Trump administration, advertising their overpriced programs on television.

All this will end badly, but our government is doing everything it can to forestall the day of judgment. In *Price v. US Department of Education*, a case recently decided in Texas, the DOE took six years to make the erroneous decision that a University of Phoenix graduate was not entitled to have her loans forgiven.[9] The DOE's ruling

---

8 Michael Corkery and Stacy Cowley, "Household Debt Makes a Comeback in the U.S.," *New York Times*, May 17, 2017, accessed August 5, 2017, https://www.nytimes.com/2017/05/17/business/dealbook/household-debt-united-states.html?_r=0.

9 Price v. U.S. Dep't of Education, 209 Fed. Supp. 3d 925 (S.D. Tex. 2016).

clearly violated federal law, and the Phoenix grad finally won relief in federal court.

But the DOE isn't concerned about following the law. It just wants to stall for time—knowing that a student-loan apocalypse is not far away.

Black Students and the Student-Loan Crisis: African Americans Suffer Most

• • •

JUDITH SCOTT-CLAYTON AND JING LI published a report for the Brookings Institution in 2016 on the disparity in student debt loads between blacks and whites. Essentially, Scott-Clayton and Li told us what we should already know, which is this: African Americans are suffering more from student-loan debt than whites.[1]

SCOTT-CLAYTON AND LI'S FINDINGS
Here are the report's key findings:

* Blacks graduate, on average, from college with $23,400 in college loans compared to whites, who graduate with an average debt load of $16,000.
* The disparity in debt loads between blacks and whites *nearly triples* four years after graduation. By that time, the average debt load for African Americans is $52,726, compared to $28,006 for white graduates.

---

1 Judith Scott-Clayton and Jing Li, "Black-White Disparity in Student Loan Debt More than Triples after Graduation," *Evidence Speaks Reports* 2, no. 3 (October 2016): https://www.brookings.edu/research/black-white-disparity-in-student-loan-debt-more-than-triples-after-graduation/.

- Four years after graduation, black graduates are three times more likely to default on their student loans than whites. For African Americans, the rate is 7.6 percent; among whites, only 2.4 percent are in default.
- Four years after graduation, almost half of African American graduates (48 percent) owe more on their undergraduate student loans than they did when they graduated.
- African Americans are going to graduate school at higher rates than whites, but blacks are three times more likely to be in a for-profit graduate program than whites. Among whites, 9 percent enroll in for-profit graduate programs; for blacks, the rate is 28 percent.

GROWING DEBT LOADS FOR BLACK GRADUATES

In my mind, Scott-Clayton and Li's most disturbing findings are set forth in the last two bullet points. First, almost half of African American college graduates owe more on their undergraduate loans four years after graduation than they did on graduation day. What's going on?

Clearly, people who are seeing their total indebtedness grow four years after beginning the repayment phases on their loans are not making loan payments large enough to cover accruing interest. Those people either default on their loans, have loans in deferment or forbearance, or make token payments under IBRPs that are not large enough to pay down the principles on their loans.

Surely it is evident that people with growing student-loan balances four years after graduation are more likely to eventually default on their loans than people who are shrinking their loan balances.

And Scott-Clayton and Li's finding that a quarter of African American graduates students are enrolled in for-profit colleges is also alarming. We know for-profit colleges charge more than public institutions and have higher default rates and dropout rates. It should disturb us to learn that blacks are three times more likely than whites to be lured into for-profit graduate programs.

IBRPs Do Not Alleviate the High Level of Student Indebtedness among African Americans

The Obama administration and the higher-education community tout long-term IBRPs as the way to alleviate the suffering caused by crushing levels of student debt. But as Scott-Clayton and Li correctly point out, new repayment options such as REPAYE "may alleviate the worst consequences of racial debt disparities," but they fail "to address the underlying causes."[2]

Lowering monthly payments and extending the repayment period from ten years to twenty or twenty-five years does not relieve African Americans from crushing levels of student debt. We've got to shut down the for-profit college sector to eliminate the risk that people will enroll in overpriced for-profit graduate programs that are often of low quality. And we've got to fundamentally reform the federal student-loan program so that African Americans, and indeed all Americans, can graduate from college without being burdened by unreasonably high levels of debt.

---

2 Ibid.

Suicide and Student Loans: Is There a Link?

• • •

DEATH RATES AMONG WHITE, MIDDLE-AGED Americans have gone up significantly in recent years, according to a recent study by Anne Case and Angus Deaton, two Princeton economists.[1] Case and Deaton found that death rates for people in the forty-five to fifty-four age group began steadily going up beginning in 1999. For middle-aged white people with high-school diplomas or less education, the mortality rate rose 22 percent between 1999 and 2013.[2]

Why are relatively young white Americans dying at a higher rate than they did fifteen years ago? Case and Deaton say most of the rising mortality rate can be attributed to suicide or deaths related to alcohol or drug abuse.[3] It seems this age group may be experiencing a lot of stress, including economic stress, and are turning to alcohol and drugs to deal with it. "What we see here is a group that's in quite a lot of distress," said Ms. Case in a *Wall Street Journal* interview.[4]

---

1 Anne Case and Angus Deaton, "Rising Morbidity and Mortality in Midlife among White Non-Hispanic Americans in the 21st Century," *PNAS* 112, no. 49 (December 2015): 15078–15083, accessed August 5, 2017, http://www.pnas.org/content/early/2015/10/29/1518393112.full.pdf.

2 Ibid.

3 Ibid.

4 Betsy McKay, "The Death Rate Is Rising for Middle-Aged Whites," *Wall Street Journal*, November 3, 2015, http://www.wsj.com/articles/the-death-rate-is-rising-for-middle-aged-whites-1446499495.

Case and Deaton said in their report that "although the epidemic of pain, suicide, and drug overdoses preceded the financial crisis, ties to economic insecurity are possible. After the productivity slowdown in the early 1970s, and with widening income inequality, many of the baby-boom generation are the first to find, in midlife, that they will not be better off than were their parents. Growth in real median earnings has been slow for this group, especially those with only a high school education."[5]

As everyone knows, Americans' accumulated student-loan debt has been going up steadily over the past thirty years. Could there be a link between student-loan debt and rising mortality rates among middle-aged white Americans?

Deaton and Case did not examine student-loan indebtedness in their study, and any attempt to link student loans to rising death rates would be speculative. Moreover, Case and Deaton found that middle-aged people with college degrees had not experienced higher mortality rates.

Nevertheless, suicide rates for the Baby Boomer generation have gone up dramatically in recent years. According to a report by Katherine Hempstead and Julie Phillips, the suicide rate for people in the forty to sixty-four age group has gone up 40 percent since 2007.[6]

Hempstead and Philips suggest that economic problems may have contributed to the rising suicide rate among baby boomers, and that "adverse effects of economic difficulties on psychological well-being may have been greater for those who did not anticipate them;

5 Anne Case and Angus Deaton, "Rising Morbidity and Mortality in Midlife among White Non-Hispanic Americans in the 21st Century," *PNAS* 112, no. 49 (December 2015): 15078–15083, accessed August 5, 2017, http://www.pnas.org/content/early/2015/10/29/1518393112.full.pdf.

6 Katherine A. Hempstead and Julie A. Phillips, "Rising Suicide among Adults Aged 40–64 Years: The Role of Job and Financial Circumstances," *American Journal of Preventive Medicine* 84, no. 5 (2015): 491–500, http://www.ajpmonline.org/article/S0749-3797 (14)00662-X/pdf.

this may well have been the case for those who were educated and wealthier..."[7]

One thing is certain: our federal government has constructed a student-loan scheme so heartless that it almost seems to have been designed to plunge millions of Americans into long-term clinical depressions. So isn't it reasonable to conclude that there is some connection between crushing student loans and rising suicide rates among middle-aged people?

Let's examine some of the evidence pointing to growing stress among student-loan debtors:

* The *New York Times* recently pointed out that ten million people are in default on their student loans or delinquent on their loan payments.[8]
* A 2015 report by two Brookings Institution researchers said that loan balances for a significant number of student-loan debtors *actually went up* after they entered the repayment phases of their loans.[9] Why? Because a lot of people obtain economic-hardship deferments that exempt them from making loan payments due to dire economic circumstances. But because they are not paying down accruing interest, their loan balances are getting larger, making them more difficult to pay off.

---

7 Ibid.

8 "Why Student Debtors Go Unrescued," *New York Times*, October 7, 2015, accessed August 5, 2017, http://www.nytimes.com/2015/10/07/opinion/why-student-debtors-go-unrescued.html?_r=0.

9 Adam Looney and Constantine Yannelis, *A Crisis in Student Loans? How Changes in the Characteristics of Borrowers and in the Institutions They Attended Contributed to Rising Default Rates*. Washington, DC: Brookings Institution, 2015). https://www.brookings.edu/bpea-articles/a-crisis-in-student-loans-how-changes-in-the-characteristics-of-borrowers-and-in-the-institutions-they-attended-contributed-to-rising-loan-defaults/.

* The percentage of elderly Americans with unpaid student-loan debt is going up. According to a report from the Government Accountability Office, the percentage of people in the sixty-five through seventy-four age group with outstanding student loans grew from 1 percent in 2004 to 4 percent in 2010, a four-fold increase. And the amount of student-loan debt owed by elderly people is growing as well. In fact, the amount of debt held by elderly Americans grew six fold between 2005 and 2013—from $2.8 billion in 2005 to $18.2 billion.[10]

* The federal government is garnishing more and more Social Security checks to collect on unpaid student loans. In 2002, only 31,000 people had Social Security benefits garnished because they had defaulted on their student loans. That number ballooned fivefold in just eleven years. In 2013, 155,000 Americans saw their Social Security checks reduced due to unpaid student-loans.

Let's consider that last bullet point from a more personal perspective. According to a story posed on *Market Watch*, the US government is garnishing the Social Security checks of Naomia Davis, an eighty-year-old woman who is suffering from advanced Alzheimer's disease. Ms. Davis's only income is her $894 Social Security check, and the feds take $134 of it to pay down on an old student loan.[11]

---

10 US Government Accountability Office, *Older Americans: Inability to Repay Student Loans May Affect Financial Security of a Small Percentage of Borrowers*, (Washington, DC: Government Accountability Office), http://www.gao.gov/products/GAO-14-866T.

11 Jillian Berman, "When Your Social Security Check Disappears Because of an Old Student Loan," *MarketWatch*, June 25, 2015, http://www.marketwatch.com/story/when-your-social-security-check-disappears-because-of-an-old-student-loan-2015-06-25.

In short, it is reasonable to conclude that crushing student-loan debt contributes to depression and even suicide among baby boomers who are struggling to pay off college loans they took out when they were young. The student-loan crisis is not only eroding Americans' sense of economic well-being, it may literally be killing them.

Educational Credit Management Corporation and the Department of Education Are a Couple of Bullies: The Scott Farkus Affair that Never Ends

• • •

FORTUNATELY, WE ONLY SEE SCOTT Farkus once a year. He comes around every Christmas Eve, when TBS runs *The Christmas Story* for twenty-four hours. Farkus, you remember, is the yellow-eyed bully that picks on Ralphie Parker and his little brother, Randy. Farkus is always accompanied by his pint-sized sidekick, Grover Dill.

Scott Farkus, of course, is a fictional bully, but destitute student borrowers are tormented by a real-life bully—ECMC. ECMC, a so-called fiduciary of the US DOE, gets paid well to hound student-loan debtors who naïvely try to shed their student loans in bankruptcy to get fresh starts.

Would you like some examples of ECMC's bullying behavior? Here are a few:

1. ECMC opposed bankruptcy relief for Janet Roth, a woman in her sixties with chronic health problems, who was living on a Social Security income of $774 a month.[1]
2. ECMC successfully blocked Janice Stevenson, a woman in her fifties, from discharging her student loans in bankruptcy—loans that were almost twenty-five years old. At the

---

1 Roth v. Educational Management Corp., 490 B. R. 908 (B.A.P. 9th Cir. 2013).

time Stevenson filed for bankruptcy, she was living on about $1,000 a month and had a history of homelessness.[2]

3. A bankruptcy judge slapped ECMC with punitive damages in 2016 for repeatedly garnishing the wages of Kristin Bruner-Halteman, a bankrupt student debtor who worked at Starbucks. ECMC violated the automatic stay provision more than thirty times, the bankruptcy court ruled. And how much money was at stake? Ms. Bruner-Halteman only owed about $5,000.[3]

So Scott Farkus, in a corporate form, is alive and well in American bankruptcy courts. And Grover Dill, Farkus's little toady, is also alive and well. The DOE itself bullies student borrowers in bankruptcy, almost as cruelly as ECMC does. And here are a few examples:

4. In *Myhre v. Department of Education*, the DOE fought Bradley Myhre, an insolvent quadriplegic who tried to discharge a modest student loan in bankruptcy. The DOE lost that one. The court commended Myhre for his courage: he was working full time, but he had to employ a caregiver to feed and dress him and drive him to work.[4]

5. In *Abney v. US Department of Education*, the DOE tried unsuccessfully to persuade a Missouri bankruptcy court to deny bankruptcy relief to Michael Abney, a single father in his forties who was living on $1,300 a month and was so poor he rode a bicycle to work because he couldn't afford a car.[5]

---

2 Stevenson v. Educational Credit Management Corp., 463 B. R. 586 (Bankr. D. Mass. 2011), *aff'd*, 475 B. R. 286 (D. Mass. 2012).

3 Bruner-Halteman v. Educational Credit Management Corporation, Case No. 12-324-HDH-13, ADV. No. 14-03041, 2016 WL 1427085 (Bankr. N. D. Tex. April 8, 2016).

4 Myhre v. US Department of Education, 503 B. R. 698 (Bankr. W. D. Wis. 2013).

5 Abney v. US Department of Education, 540 B. R. 681 (Bankr. W. D. Mo. 2015).

6. In the case of *Fern v. FedLoan Servicing*, the Eighth Circuit's Bankruptcy Appellate Panel ruled against the DOE, which had tried to keep Sara Fern from discharging her student debt in bankruptcy. Fern is a single mother of three children who takes home $1,500 a month from her job and supplements her income with food stamps and public rent assistance.[6]

Have I described bullying behavior by ECMC and the DOE? Of course I have. Virtually every time the DOE or ECMC shows up in bankruptcy court, the argument is the same: "This deadbeat doesn't deserve bankruptcy relief, Your Honor. Put the worthless son of a b——tch in a twenty- or twenty-five-year IBRP."

In the past, bankruptcy courts were persuaded by these callous arguments, but judges are beginning to return to their duty. I predict the day is soon coming when the federal appellate courts will overrule the precedents that have favored ECMC and the DOE for so many years. Indeed, in recent years, the federal courts have begun to rule more compassionately in favor of distressed student-loan debtors.[7]

But for now, the bullying goes on. Just like Scott Farkus and Grover Dill, ECMC and the DOE lie in wait for hapless debtors who stagger into bankruptcy court. ECMC has accumulated $1 billion in unrestricted assets while engaging in this shameful behavior, and the federal government pays ECMC's legal fees.[8]

---

6 Fern v. FedLoan Servicing, 563 B. R. 1 (B.A.P. 8th Cir.2017).

7 See, for example, Fern v. FedLoan Servicing, 563 B. R. 1 (B.A.P. 8th Cir.2017); Krieger v. Educational Credit Management Corporation, 713 F.3d 882 (7th Cir. 2013); Roth v. Educational Credit Management Corporation, 490 B. R. 908 (B.A.P. 9th Cir. 2013); Educational Credit Management Corporation v. Polleys, 356 F.3d 1302 (10th Cir. 2004).

8 Robert Shireman and Tariq Habash, *Have Student Loan Guaranty Agencies Lost Their Way?* (The Century Foundation: September 29, 2016), accessed August 5, 2017, https://tcf.org/content/report/student-loan-guaranty-agencies-lost-way/.

Tax Consequences for Student-Loan Borrowers in Income-Based Repayment Plans Are Insanity

• • •

THE STUDENT-LOAN CRISIS GROWS WORSE with each passing day. As the *Wall Street Journal* noted recently, total student-loan indebtedness is more than five times what it was just twenty years ago, and one out of four borrowers is behind on repayment or in default.[1]

But American universities survive on federal student-aid money; they are like addicts waiting on their next fix. Tuition rates continue to go up: Yale recently announced a tuition hike to nearly $50,000 a year![2]

The Obama administration knew the student-loan program was out of control, but the only thing it could think of to do was roll out IBRPs that stretch borrowers' payments out for twenty or twenty-five years. More than 5 million people are in these plans now, and the DOE wants 7 million people in them by the end of 2017. I think there will eventually be 10 million people in these plans.

---

1 Anne Tergesen, "Six Common Mistakes People Make with Their Student Loans," *Wall Street Journal*, September 12, 2016, accessed August 5, 2017, http://www.wsj.com/articles/six-common-mistakes-people-make-with-their-student-loans-1473645782.

2 "Yale Financial Aid Budget Will Meet Term Bill Increase," *Yale News*, March 9, 2016, accessed August 5, 2017, http://news.yale.edu/2016/03/09/yale-financial-aid-budget-will-meet-term-bill-increase.

IBRPs reduce borrowers' monthly payments because borrowers' payment terms are based on percentages of their incomes—not the amounts they borrowed. In Obama's two IBRP plans—PAYE and REPAYE—borrowers pay 10 percent of their discretionary incomes for twenty years.

But this is insanity. For most borrowers in PAYE and REPAYE, monthly payments are not large enough to cover accruing interest, and total indebtedness actually grows larger over the years as accruing interest gets added to the amount that was originally borrowed.

It is true that borrowers who faithfully make loan payments for twenty years will have the remaining loan balances forgiven, but the amount of forgiven debt is considered taxable income by the IRS. In fact, a *Wall Street Journal* article advised borrowers to start saving their money to pay the tax bill they will receive when they finish paying off their loans.

Alan Moore, a financial planner who was quoted in the *WSJ*, made this chilling observation: "If you don't save enough money for the tax bill, all you are accomplishing is swapping your student-loan debt for a debt to the IRS." Moore advised student-loan borrowers to open segregated accounts to save for their eventual tax bills and not to invest that money too aggressively due to the risk of a bear market.

Higher education insiders[3] chant the mantra that people who get college degrees make more money than people who don't go to college. But that is not true for everyone. And that trite observation does not justify forcing millions of people into twenty- and twenty-five-year repayment plans that terminate with big tax bills that come due just about the time most Americans hope to retire.

---

3 Press release of U.S. Department of Education, "FACT SHEET: A College Degree: Surest Pathway to Expanded Opportunity, Success for American Students," September 16, 2016, accessed August 6, 2016, https://www.highbeam.com/doc/1P3-4184751381.html.

The Student-Loan Crisis Is Worse than the 2008 Housing Crisis: The Return of *The Big Short*

• • •

As EVERYONE KNOWS, THE HOUSING market collapsed in 2008, triggering a major economic crisis in the United States. The nation descended into recession, and the national economy is still recovering from this catastrophe.

Steve Rhode and others have described a student-loan bubble, and I share these commentators' view that the federal student-loan program as it functions now is unsustainable.[1] Approximately 42 million borrowers collectively owe $1.4 trillion in student-loan debt, and families are beginning to experience sticker shock. Enrollments are declining at the for-profit schools, and nonprofit liberal-arts colleges are desperately scrambling to maintain their enrollments.

Many people may think the student-loan crisis—no matter how bad it is—is just a small tremor compared to the 2008 housing crisis, which was an earthquake. But in fact, the student-loan crisis has produced more casualties in terms of human suffering than the housing collapse did ten years ago.

---

1 Steve Rhode, "The Student Loan Bubble That Many Don't Want to See," *Get Out Of Debt Guy* (blog), July 15, 2016, accessed August 6, 2017, https://get-outofdebt.org/99519/student-loan-bubble-many-dont-want-see; Jill Schlesinger, "Looking for the Next Bubble," *Chicago Tribune*, August 24, 2016, accessed August 5, 2017, http://www.chicagotribune.com/business/sns-201608241800--tms--retiresmctnrs-a20160824-20160824-story.html.

Alan White of *Credit Slip*, an online news source on economic matters, recently commented on a housing-data report released by the Urban Institute. Based on the Urban Institute's data, White assessed the total damage from the subprime housing crisis. From 2007 to 2016, 6.7 million homes went into foreclosure, and another 2 million homes were lost through short sales or deeds in lieu of foreclosure.[2] Thus, the total number of homeowners who lost their homes in the subprime housing debacle is about 8.7 million. If we assume a majority of those homes were owned by married couples, then the total number of individuals who were injured in the housing crisis is about 17 million.

That's a lot of people, but the casualty list from the student-loan crisis is larger. As the *New York Times* reported in 2015, about 10 million student borrowers have defaulted on their loans or have loans in delinquency.[3] Almost 6 million debtors are now in IDRs, and those people are locked into repayment plans that last from twenty to twenty-five years. A majority of those people are making payments so low they are not servicing accruing interest, which means their student-loan balances are growing larger (negatively amortizing) with each passing month.

So, we're talking about 16 million people who have defaulted, have delinquent loans, or who are in IDRs. And millions more have student loans in forbearance or deferment, which means they are not making payments on their loans but are not counted as defaulters. For most of those people, interest is accruing, which means their student-loan balances are growing. The Consumer Financial Protection Bureau reported a total of nearly 9 million people in

---

2 Alan White, "Foreclosure Crisis Update," *Credit Slip*, April 5, 2017, accessed August 5, 2017, http://www.creditslips.org/creditslips/2017/04/foreclosure-crisis-update.html?

3 "Why Student Debtors Go Unrescued," *New York Times*, October 7, 2015, accessed August 5, 2017, http://www.nytimes.com/2015/10/07/opinion/why-student-debtors-go-unrescued.html?_r=0.

deferment or forbearance in its 2013 report titled *A Closer Look at the Trillion.*[4]

All these numbers are fluid. Some delinquent student-loan borrowers will bring their loans current, and some defaulters will rehabilitate their loans. And some people will move from deferment status to some form of IDR.

But it is safe to say—indeed conservative to say—that about 20 million Americans have outstanding student loans they can't pay back. That's 3 million more people that were injured by the housing crisis. It's *The Big Short* all over again.

Alan and Catherine Murray, who received a partial discharge of their student loans in a Kansas bankruptcy court in 2016, are the poster children for this calamity. They borrowed $77,000 to finance their studies, and each obtained a bachelor's degree and a master's degree. They paid back $54,000—about 70 percent of what they borrowed.

But the Murrays experienced hard times and put their loans into deferment for a few years while interest accrued at the rate of 9 percent. They now owe $311,000! Will they ever pay that back? No, they won't.[5]

Yes, the federal loan program is in a bubble, and the suffering has already begun. The federal government is propping up this house of cards and disguising the real default rate. Congress doesn't have the courage to address the problem, and the Trump administration appears to be clueless. Stay tuned for further developments.

---

4 Rohit Chopra, "A Closer Look at the Trillion," *Consumer Financial Protection Bureau* (blog), August 5, 2013, https://www.consumerfinance.gov/about-us/blog/a-closer-look-at-the-trillion/.

5 Murray v. Educational Credit Management Corp., 563 B.R. 52 (Bankr. D. Kan. 2016).

It Seemed Like a Good Idea at the Time: Student-Loan Forgiveness Programs are Making the Student-Loan Crisis Worse

• • •

THE FEDERAL GOVERNMENT'S STUDENT-LOAN FORGIVENESS programs—like Germany's decision to invade Russia in 1941—must have seemed like a good idea at the time.

After all, millions of college students are burdened by crushing student loans, the student-loan default rate creeps ever upward, and many college graduates have not gotten jobs that pay well enough to service their student-loan debts.

So why not create some programs that will lower student borrowers' monthly loan payments? And so the government created two programs that are essentially student-loan forgiveness programs. One program allows people who take public-service jobs to make loan payments based on percentages of their incomes for ten years. At the end of the ten-year period, the balances of their loans are forgiven.

The other program—IBRP—allows borrowers to make monthly student-loan payments based on percentages of their incomes for twenty or twenty-five years (there are several variations). Just as with the public-service loan-forgiveness plans, student-loan debtors will see the balances of their loans forgiven at the end of the repayment periods.

The attractiveness of these programs for student-loan borrowers is obvious. They see their monthly payments go down, which may keep many student-loan debtors from going into default.

But there is a downside. Neither of these programs contain provisions to discourage students from borrowing more money than necessary. In fact—since the monthly payments are based on a percentage of the borrower's income and not the amount borrowed, the programs contain a perverse incentive to borrow as much as possible. As a result, many of the people making income-based loan payments will never pay back even a portion of their loans. Here are a couple of examples—one taken from a *Wall Street Journal* article and one taken from a *New York Times* story—that illustrate the problem.

Haley Schafer borrowed $312,000 to attend veterinary school in the Caribbean. Even though the job market for veterinarians in the United States is terrible, Schafer got a job making about $60,000 a year, which wasn't nearly enough to comfortably pay back her student loans under the standard ten-year repayment plan.

So Schafer signed up for a twenty-five-year IBRP that lowered her monthly loan payments to about $400 a month. Unfortunately, her monthly payments aren't large enough to cover accruing interest on her loans. The *New York Times* estimated that her loan balance will continue to grow, and when she finishes her twenty-five-year repayment plan, her loan balance will be more than twice the amount that she borrowed—$650,000.[1]

And that's Haley Schafer's story. Now, let's hear about Max Norris, a public-service attorney who borrowed $172,000 to go to University of California's Hastings College of Law.[2] Under the

1 David Segal, "High Debt and Falling Demand Trap New Vets," *New York Times*, February 23, 2013, accessed August 5, 2017, http://www.nytimes.com/2013/02/24/business/high-debt-and-falling-demand-trap-new-veterinarians.html.

2 Josh Mitchell, "Student-Debt Forgiveness Plans Skyrocket, Raising Fears Over Costs, Higher Tuition," *Wall Street Journal*, April 22, 2014, accessed

public-service student-loan forgiveness plan, he only pays $420 a month on his loan balance, not enough to cover accruing interest.

Norris's loan balance will be forgiven after ten years. Assuming Norris stays in public service and gets annual raises of 4 percent, the government will forgive $225,000 in student-loan indebtedness—more than Norris borrowed!

In other words, the federal government is giving Morris a 100 percent subsidy to go to law school, even though the market is flooded with lawyers. In fact, there are currently two law-school graduates for every new legal job.

Surely, anyone can see that it makes no sense for the federal government to permit people to borrow $100,000 or more to train for professions that are already overcrowded and then allow them to make loan payments that are so small that the payments don't cover the accruing interest.

But that is what our federal government is doing.

And although creative repayment programs may help keep the student-loan default rate down, they are actually making the student-loan crisis worse. Not only do we have 8 million people who have stopped making loan payments and are in default, we have millions more who aren't making payments because they received an economic hardship deferment or are entitled to some other form of forbearance. And then we have more than 5 million people who are making loan payments based not on the amounts they borrowed but on their incomes, which means most will never pay off the principals of their loans. In short—the number of people who will never pay off their student loans is in the millions—many, many millions.

August 6, 2017, https://www.wsj.com/articles/plans-that-forgive-student-debt-skyrocket-raising-fears-over-costs-1398126083/.

The Deepwater Horizon Syndrome:
The Department of Education Ignores Signs
of an Impending Student-Loan Meltdown

• • •

DEEPWATER HORIZON, A GIANT OFFSHORE drilling rig in the Gulf of Mexico, blew out on April 20, 2010. Eleven workers died, and more than 200 million gallons of crude oil spewed into the Gulf.

According to the recent film about the blowout,[1] this catastrophe could have been prevented. Instruments on the rig alerted workers that pressure was building around the concrete core and that a blowout was imminent, but supervisors convinced themselves that the instruments were malfunctioning and everything was fine.

Something similar is happening with the student-loan crisis. The DOE issued its college scorecard in 2015, which reported the percentage of students who are in repayment and actually paying down their loans. The DOE reported that 61.1 percent of student borrowers had made some progress toward paying down their loan balances five years into repayment.[2] But a coding error led to an erroneous

---

1 *Deepwater Horizon*, directed by Peter Berg (2016, Summit Entertainment).

2 Michael Stratford, "The New College Scorecard," *Inside Higher Ed*, September 14, 2015, accessed August 5, 2017, https://www.insidehighered.com/news/2015/09/14/obama-administration-publishes-new-college-earnings-loan-repayment-data.

report.[3] As Robert Kelchen, a professor at Seton Hall University, explained in a blog posting, the picture is much bleaker than the DOE portrayed.[4]

A revised analysis reported that less than half of student borrowers made any progress toward paying off their student loans five years into the repayment phase. Among borrowers who attended for-profit colleges, the numbers are even more startling. Five years into repayment, only about a third of for-profit students (35 percent) had reduced their loan balances by even one dollar!

People who don't reduce their loan balances five years after beginning repayment are not likely to pay off their student loans—ever. In fact, the Brookings Institution reported in 2015 that nearly half of for-profit borrowers in a recent cohort had defaulted on their loans within five years (47 percent).[5]

In short, the DOE is behaving just like the technicians in the movie *Deepwater Horizon*. The data warn of an impending blowout, but the DOE keeps pumping money to the for-profit colleges. A disaster is inevitable, and there are already millions of casualties.

---

3 Paul Fain, "Feds' Data Error Inflated Loan Repayment Rates on the College Scoreboard," *Inside Higher Ed*, January 16, 2017, accessed August 5, 2017, https://www.insidehighered.com/news/2017/01/16/feds-data-error-inflated-loan-repayment-rates-college-scorecard.

4 Robert Kelchen, "How Much Did a Coding Error Affect Student Loan Repayment Rates?" *Kelchen on Education* (blog), January 13, 2017, accessed August 5, 2017, https://kelchenoneducation.wordpress.com/2017/01/13/how-much-did-a-coding-error-affect-student-loan-repayment-rates/.

5 Adam Looney and Constantine Yannelis, *A Crisis in Student Loans? How Changes in the Characteristics of Borrowers and in the Institutions They Attended Contributed to Rising Default Rates* (Washington, DC: Brookings Institution, 2015), https://www.brookings.edu/bpea-articles/a-crisis-in-student-loans-how-changes-in-the-characteristics-of-borrowers-and-in-the-institutions-they-attended-contributed-to-rising-loan-defaults/.

California Bar Exam Pass Rate Hits Thirty-Two-Year Low, But Law-School Graduates Who Fail the Bar Exam Must Still Pay Off Their Student Loans

• • •

IN JULY 2016, 7,737 PEOPLE sat for the California bar exam, and only 3,332 test takers passed—a 43 percent pass rate. A total of 4,405 people—57 percent of test takers—failed the exam, which is the lowest pass rate since 1984.[1]

In all fifty states, JD graduates cannot practice law until they pass a bar exam. Thus, the 4,405 law graduates who failed the California bar exam last July suffered a major setback in their professional careers.

They also suffered a financial catastrophe. The average JD graduate leaves law school with more than $100,000 in student-loan debt,[2] and that debt must be paid regardless of whether the graduate passes a bar exam or ever gets a job as a lawyer. Without a doubt,

---

1 Ann Yarbrough, "Bar Exam Pass Rate Dips to 32-Year Low," *California Bar Journal*, (December 2016), accessed August 6, 2017, http://www.calbarjournal. com/December2016/TopHeadlines/TH2.aspx.

2 Noam Scheiber, "An Expensive Law Degree and No Place to Use It," *New York Times*, June 17, 2016, accessed August 5, 2017, http://www.nytimes. com/2016/06/19/business/dealbook/an-expensive-law-degree-and-no-place-to-use-it.html?_r=0.

the majority of the people who failed the California bar exam in July 2016 have student-loan debt.

Obviously, the risk of failing the bar is not equally distributed among test takers. People who graduate from schools accredited by the American Bar Association have higher pass rates on the California bar exam than people who attend a law school that is only accredited by the state of California. Sixty percent of test takers who graduated from out-of-state ABA-accredited schools passed the July bar exam, while only 21 percent of people who attended state-accredited schools passed.

And people who fail the bar exam the first time they take it have a lower pass rate than overall test takers if they retake the exam. Among exam repeaters, only 17 percent passed the California bar exam last July. Those are pretty bad odds.

The California bar exam results are just another indication that the future for many law-school graduates is bleak. The legal job market has less than six lawyer jobs for every ten new law graduates,[3] and it offers no law jobs for graduates who cannot pass the bar. People who graduate high in their classes from prestigious law schools such as Harvard or Stanford are eminently employable, but people who graduate in the bottom halves of their classes or who attend bottom-tier law schools may never obtain a job that will justify the student-loan debt they piled up to get a law degree.

So, if you are thinking about going to law school, here's my advice. Read Paul Campos's book titled *Don't Go to Law School (Unless)*. And ponder Campos's observation that "somewhere around four out of

---

3 Kyle McEntee, "Law Grads Still Face Tough a Job Market," *Bloomberg Law*, May 4, 2016, accessed August 5, 2017, https://bol.bna.com/law-grads-still-face-a-tough-job-market/.

five current law students would be better off if they hadn't gone to law school." [4]

And if you went to law school, can't find a law job, and are unable to pay off your student loans, you should consider bankruptcy. But if you go that route and try to get your law-school loans discharged, you must educate the bankruptcy judge about the terrible job market for lawyers.

---

4 Paul Campos, *Don't Go To Law School (Unless)*, (Lexington, KY: CreateSpace Independent Publishing Platform, 2012), xiii.

Bankrupt Student-Loan Debtors Need Good Lawyers: The Sad Case of *Ronald Joe Johnson v. US Department of Education*

• • •

WE OFTEN HEAR THAT STUDENT loans cannot be discharged in bankruptcy—-don't even try. But in fact, quite a few people have gotten relief from their student loans in the bankruptcy courts. And a few student-loan debtors have gone to bankruptcy court without lawyers and been successful.

But if you go to bankruptcy court to shed your student loans, you should bring a good attorney because the DOE or one of its agents will be there to meet you, and the DOE and its proxies have battalions of skilled lawyers who will fight you every step of the way.

THE SAD CASE OF *RONALD JOE JOHNSON V. US DEPARTMENT OF EDUCATION*

Johnson v. US Department of Education, decided in 2015, illustrates why student-loan debtors should have good lawyers to represent them in the bankruptcy courts. In that case, Judge Tamara Mitchell, an Alabama bankruptcy judge, refused to discharge Ronald Joe Johnson's student loans even though he and his wife were living on the edge of poverty.[1] If Mr. Johnson had been represented by a competent attorney, I think he might have won his case.

In 2015, Johnson filed an adversary proceeding in an Alabama bankruptcy court, seeking to have his student loans discharged. The US DOE opposed a discharge (as it almost always does), and a lawyer from the US Attorney's Office in Birmingham, Alabama, showed up to represent the DOE and make sure Johnson lost his case.

Johnson had taken out student loans in the 1990s to enroll in some sort of postsecondary program that Judge Mitchell did not bother to describe in her opinion. Johnson testified that he had enrolled for four semesters but had only completed one of them. He testified further that his studies had not benefited him at all.

In 2000, Johnson obtained a direct consolidation loan in the amount of about $25,000, with interest accruing at 8.25 percent per year. Although he paid approximately $10,000 on the loan, mostly through wage garnishments and tax offsets, he hadn't reduced the principal by even one dollar. In fact, when Johnson appeared in bankruptcy court in 2015, his debt had grown to over $41,000.

Mr. Johnson desperately needed relief from his student loans. He testified at trial that he made about $2,000 a month working at two jobs; he was a municipal employee and also an employee at a local Walmart. His wife suffered from diabetes, which required expenditures for insulin and other supplies, and of course, some of his income had been garnished by the government.

Unfortunately for Mr. Johnson, he signed a formal stipulation of facts that a DOE lawyer had cunningly prepared. In that stipulation, Johnson affirmed that it would not be an undue hardship for him to repay his student loans.

Although Mr. Johnson did not know it at the time, he lost his adversary proceeding the instant he signed his name to the DOE's

---

1 Johnson v. US Department of Education, 541 B. R. 750 (Bankr. N. D. Ala. 2015).

prepared stipulation. Debtors cannot discharge their student loans in bankruptcy unless they can show undue hardship, and Mr. Johnson admitted in writing that paying back his loans would not be an undue hardship.

In short, Johnson was a sitting duck when he walked into Judge Mitchell's bankruptcy court without legal counsel. Judge Mitchell noted that he had admitted that his loans did not present an undue hardship and that he had not brought any evidence of the expenses he had incurred to treat his wife's diabetes.

And then Judge Mitchell walked Johnson through the three-pronged *Brunner* test and concluded that he failed all three prongs.[2] He was able to pay back his loans and maintain a minimal standard of living, Judge Mitchell ruled, and he had not shown any additional circumstances indicating he could not pay back the loans in the future.

Finally, Judge Mitchell ruled that Johnson failed the good-faith prong of the *Brunner* test because he had made virtually no loan payments other than payments made through income-tax offsets and wage garnishments.

Mr. Johnson had gone to court to argue reasonably that he believed he had paid down his loans through income-tax offsets and wage garnishments. All he asked for was relief from the interest and penalties that had been added to his debt.

---

2 Brunner v. New York State Higher Education Services Corporation, 831 F.2d 395, 396 (2d Cir. 1987). The Second Circuit Court of Appeals adopted a three-prong test for determining whether a student-loan debtor will experience "undue hardship" if required to repay his or her student loans. To obtain an undue hardship discharge of student loans, the debtor must show: "(1) that the debtor cannot maintain, based on current income and expenses, a 'minimal' standard of living for herself and her dependents if forced to repay the loans; (2) that additional circumstances exist indicating that this state of affairs is likely to persist for a significant portion of the repayment period of the student loans; and (3) that the debtor has made good faith efforts to repay the loans."

But Johnson's arguments fell on deaf ears. He and his wife are stuck with a debt that grows larger every day and will probably never be repaid.

If Ronald Joe Johnson had been represented by a lawyer, he would never have signed that document. Moreover, a lawyer would have told him to bring evidence to court documenting his wife's medical expenses.

The Reasons Student Debtors Can't Find Good Lawyers

Why can't people like Ronald Joe Johnson find good lawyers to represent them in bankruptcy court? There are at least three reasons:

1. Lawyers are expensive, and people who go to bankruptcy court don't have money to hire good lawyers.
2. Bankruptcy lawyers are not keeping up with recent trends in the bankruptcy courts, and many believe—incorrectly— that it is impossible to discharge student loans in bankruptcy. Thus, even if Mr. Johnson had had money to pay a lawyer, a bankruptcy attorney might have told him that it would be pointless to try to shed his student loans in bankruptcy.
3. Legal-aid clinics and poverty-law centers, which should be representing people like Mr. Johnson, aren't interested in the student-loan crisis. They would prefer to provide pro bono legal services in landlord-tenant disputes or fight courthouse battles over traditional civil-rights issues.

Distressed student-loan debtors need legal representation in the bankruptcy courts, but they are not likely to get it. Nevertheless, some bankruptcy judges have begun issuing sensible, compassionate, and well-reasoned decisions on behalf of people like Ronald Joe Johnson. Unfortunately for Mr. Johnson, Judge Tamara Mitchell is not a compassionate bankruptcy judge.

Restaurant Chains Can File for Bankruptcy If They Borrow Too Much Money—But the Bankruptcy Courts Are Virtually Closed to Distressed Student-Loan Debtors

● ● ●

A LEAST FOUR LARGE RESTAURANT chains filed for bankruptcy in 2016—a sign perhaps that the economy is slipping back into recession.[1] Companies that own Logan's Road House, Fox & Hound, and Johnny Carino's were among the casualties.

Craig Weichmann, an investment consultant who specializes in restaurants, was quoted in a news article as saying that bankrupt restaurant chains are burdened by high debt loads and lagging same-store sales. Restaurant chains took advantage of low interest rates to borrow a lot of money, but older restaurants are losing customers to new chains. Now the old chains can't manage their debt.

But, hey, bankruptcy can be a good thing for businesses that borrow too much money. "In [the] old days, filing for bankruptcy was the end of the world," Weichmann explained. "In reality, there comes a time when filing for bankruptcy permits a group to come out sustainable and healthy." In fact, Weichmann said, a lot of companies come out of bankruptcy "with a new life."

---

1 Korri Kezar, "Why a Dallas Restaurant Company's Bankruptcy Is Part of a Trend," WFAA.com, August 10, 2016, accessed August 5, 2017, http://www.wfaa.com/news/local/dallas-county/why-a-dallas-restaurant-companys-bankruptcy-is-part-of-a-trend/293988701?

Is the United States a great country or what? Business owners who borrow money recklessly while paying themselves nice salaries can stiff their creditors by filing for bankruptcy without changing their lifestyles at all.

In fact, restaurant owners can file for bankruptcy repeatedly. Johnny Carino's owners filed for bankruptcy a second time only three months after emerging from an earlier bankruptcy. According to the *Austin Business Journal*, the company "owed $19 million to its creditors and roughly $905,000 in back wages, vacation time and bonuses to its employees, plus back taxes and lease obligations."[2]

Yes, America is truly a great country—unless you are a student-loan debtor. Although some bankruptcy judges respond humanely when destitute student-loan debtors file for bankruptcy, other courts give them a chilly reception. Even college borrowers who received no benefits from their college experiences and can't land decent jobs often find it very difficult to discharge their student loans in bankruptcy.

Brenda Butler, whose bankruptcy case was decided in 2016, is a case in point. She borrowed a modest amount of money to get a degree from Chapman College (a reputable institution in California), and she made good-faith efforts to pay off her loans for almost twenty years. But a bankruptcy court in Illinois refused to discharge her student-loan debt, which had more than doubled in size since she graduated, and it forced to her to remain in an IBRP that obligates her to make loan payments until 2037![3]

Poor Ms. Butler. Instead of going to college, she should have borrowed money to start a restaurant.

---

2 Michael Theis, "Italian Restaurant Chain Again Files for Bankruptcy," *Austin Business Journal*, July 27, 2016, accessed August 5, 2017, http://www.bizjournals.com/austin/news/2016/07/27/italian-restaurant-chain-files-again-for.html.

3 Butler v. Educational Credit Management Corp., Adv. No. 124-07069, 2016 WL 360697 (Bankr. C. D. Ill. Jan. 27, 2016).

Bankruptcy Relief Bill H. R. 2366, The Discharge Student Loans in Bankruptcy Act of 2017: Does It Have a Prayer of Becoming Law?

• • •

IN MAY 2017, CONGRESSMEN JOHN Delaney (D–Maryland) and John Katko (R–New York) filed a bill in the House of Representatives that would eliminate the undue-hardship rule contained in 11 U. S. C. sec. 523(a)(8). H. R. 2366, titled the Discharge Student Loans in Bankruptcy Act, if adopted into law, would put student loans on par with credit-card debt and other consumer debt, making student loans more easily dischargeable in bankruptcy. As Congressman Delaney explained in a press release, "It doesn't make sense for students with heavy debt burdens to be worse off than someone with credit card debt or mortgage debt."[1]

HOW MANY STUDENT BORROWERS WOULD BENEFIT IF DELANEY-KATKO BILL BECOMES LAW?

The Delaney-Katko Bill would be a very big deal if it becomes law. If the undue-hardship rule is struck from the Bankruptcy Code,

---

1 "Delaney and Katko File Legislation to Help Americans Struggling with Student Loan Debt," May 5, 2017, accessed August 5, 2017, https://delaney.house.gov/news/press-releases/delaney-and-katko-file-legislation-to-help-americans-struggling-with-student.

millions of student borrowers could seek relief from their student loans. How many millions?

We know from looking at a 2015 Brookings Institution report that nearly half the people from a recent cohort of borrowers who took out student loans to attend for-profit colleges defaulted within five years. Clearly, a great many of these people would qualify for bankruptcy relief.

And the Federal Reserve Bank of New York reported recently that a third of student borrowers who owed $5,000 or less defaulted in five years, while 18 percent of the people who borrowed $100,000 or more defaulted. Assuming these defaulters are insolvent, nearly all of them will be eligible for bankruptcy relief if the Delaney-Katko bill becomes law.

Who Will Oppose This Legislation?

Obviously, most of the 44 million people weighed down by student-loan debt will support this bill. Who will oppose it?

The bill would give bankruptcy relief for people who took out both federal student loans and private student loans. Private lenders who are heavily invested in the student-loan business—Wells Fargo, Sallie Mae, and so on—can be expected to oppose this bill fiercely, and their lobbyists may already be at work.

The nation's colleges and universities will also oppose this bill, but they won't be vocal about it. It is hard for universities to insist on getting billions of dollars in federal student-aid money every year while publicly opposing relief to people who went broke because they borrowed too much money to attend college.

But make no mistake: the colleges and universities understand that the Delaney-Katko bill, if it becomes law, will unleash a floodgate of bankruptcy filings, and this deluge will force Congress to clean up the student-loan scandal. The colleges want the party to last a little while longer, and this legislation will help bring the party to an end if it ever gets enacted.

In the past, beneficiaries of the student-loan boondoggle have used lobbyists and campaign contributions very effectively to protect their interests, while student debtors suffered in silence. But the tables may be about to turn. More than 40 million people are burdened by student-loan debt, and these people vote.

WILL THE DELANEY-KATKO BILL BECOME LAW?

What are the chances that the Delaney-Katko bill will become law? It is hard to say. A bill was introduced several years ago to stop the government from garnishing the Social Security checks of student-loan defaulters, and that bill never made it out of committee.

So it is possible that this bill will go nowhere. Nevertheless, I am impressed by the fact that the Delaney-Katko bill has been framed as a bipartisan initiative. So far, it has at least ten cosponsors:

* Debbie Dingell (D–Michigan)
* Paul Tonko (D–New York)
* Kyrsten Lea Sinema (D-Arizona)
* Zoe Lofgren (D-California)
* John Delaney (D-Maryland)
* John Katko (R–New York)
* Edwin Perlmutter (D-Colorado)
* Alan Lowenthal (D-California)
* Catherine Castor (D-Florida)
* Marc Veasy (D-Texas)

STUDENT DEBTORS SHOULD WRITE TO THEIR ELECTED REPRESENTATIVES AND EXPRESS THEIR SUPPORT FOR THE DELANEY-KATKO BILL

The Delaney-Katko bill, if it becomes law, will afford relief to millions of people who have been pushed out of the economy by student loans. Let's watch this bill closely and give it all the support we can.

Every student-loan debtor should write his or her senator and congressperson to express support for the Delaney-Katko bill. They should stress that this proposed legislation is not radical. In fact, scholars and policy makers have advocated for years that distressed student-loan debtors should have easier access to the bankruptcy courts.

And let's take a moment to salute the political courage of Representative John Katko of New York—the first Republican to support this legislation.

Butler v. Educational Credit Management Corporation: Brenda Butler, Poster Child for the Student-Loan Crisis, Will Be Done with Her Student Loans in 2037—Forty-Two Years after She Graduated from College

• • •

IF THE STUDENT-LOAN CRISIS HAD a poster child, it might well be Brenda Butler, who lost her bankruptcy case in 2016 in Illinois.[1] Butler borrowed about $14,000 to get a degree in English and creative writing from Chapman University, which she received in 1995. Over the next twenty years, she made loan payments totaling $15,000—more than the amount she borrowed.

Unfortunately, she was unable to make payments from time to time, and her debt grew due to accrued interest and penalties. When she filed for bankruptcy in 2014, Butler's debt had grown to almost $33,000, more than twice what she borrowed!

Did Butler get rich in the twenty-one years that passed since she graduated from college? No, she didn't. When she filed for bankruptcy, she owned no real property and drove a 2001 Saturn that had logged 147,000 miles. According to the bankruptcy court, Butler never made more than about $35,000 a year, and her monthly income

---

1 Butler v. Educational Credit Management Corporation, Adv. No. 124-07069, 2016 WL 360697 (Bankr. C. D. Ill. Jan. 27, 2016).

at the time of her bankruptcy filing was only $1,879, about $300 less than her expenses.

In spite of her bleak financial situation and an employment history of relatively low wages, a bankruptcy judge refused to discharge Ms. Butler's student loans. In fact, in applying the three-pronged *Brunner* test,[2] the court ruled that she failed to meet two of the prongs.

First, the court concluded that Butler was able to maintain a minimum standard of living, in spite of the fact that she was living on unemployment benefits at the time of her hearing and those benefits were about to run out. Indeed, the court admitted that Butler "had virtually no resources to support herself."[3]

Nevertheless, in the court's view, Butler would likely find employment soon, which would enable her to maintain a minimum standard of living and make payments under an IBRP. Thus, Butler failed the first prong of the *Brunner* test.

Brunner's second prong required Butler to show that additional circumstances existed that prevented her from paying on her student loans in the future. Here again, the judge ruled against her. The judge found Butler to be "capable and intelligent with no health problems or other impediments to being gainfully employed."[4] The court acknowledged that Butler had "an unfortunate employment history through no apparent fault of her own,"[5] but she could show

---

2 Brunner v. New York State Higher Education Services Corporation, 831 F.2d 395, 396 (2d Cir. 1987). Section 523(a)(8) of the US Bankruptcy Code states that student loans are not dischargeable in bankruptcy unless the repayment of the loans would create an "undue hardship" on the debtor and the debtor's dependents. Congress did not define undue hardship, and most federal circuits have adopted the three-prong *Brunner* test to determine whether repayment of student loans would constitute an undue hardship.

3 Ibid., *4.

4 Ibid.

5 Ibid., *15.

no exceptional circumstances that would indicate that she could not pay back her student loans in the coming years.

Interestingly, the judge ruled in Butler's favor regarding one prong of the *Brunner* test. In the judge's view, Butler had met her burden of showing she had made good-faith efforts to pay back her loans. As the judge acknowledged, Butler had made payments totaling more than the original principal on her loans, and she had made diligent efforts to improve her financial status. "This is not a case of a recent graduate trying to escape student-loan debts before beginning a lucrative career," the judge admitted. On the contrary, Butler had made "substantial, though futile, efforts to pay down her student loan debt."[6]

So why did Butler lose her case? This is the bankruptcy judge's summary: "[Butler's] financial situation is unfortunate, but more than that is required for a finding of undue hardship under the demanding *Brunner* test. [Butler] has shown good faith in her efforts to remain employed and pay down her student loan debt. But as a healthy, intelligent, relatively young worker with a proven ability to secure productive employment, [she] is unable to prove that her student loan obligations prevent her from maintaining a minimum standard of living, now or in the foreseeable future. Thus…[Butler's] student loan debt will not be discharged."[7]

The *Butler* decision is particularly unfortunate because her situation is not atypical. Like a lot of people, she obtained a liberal-arts degree from a private college that never led to a well-paying job. In spite of good-faith efforts to pay back her loans, she was dragged down by relentlessly accruing interest (and perhaps by exorbitant fees), like thousands of other Americans.

---

6 Ibid., *6.
7 Ibid.

And here is the final outcome. Brenda Butler most likely will continue in a long-term IBRP that will not conclude until 2037—forty-two years after she graduated from college!

Surely this is not what Brenda Butler envisioned when she enrolled at Chapman University in 1991 with bright hopes for her future. And surely this is not what Congress envisioned when it passed the Higher Education Act more than fifty years ago.

And that is why Brenda Butler would make a good poster child for the student-loan crisis. She's a good person who went to college in good faith and made good-faith efforts to pay back her student loans, and she will be burdened with student-loan debt—mostly penalties and interest—until she reaches retirement age.

Bruner-Halteman v. Educational Credit Management Corporation: A Texas Bankruptcy Court Slaps ECMC with Punitive Damages for Repeatedly Garnishing a Starbucks Employee's Paychecks in Violation of the Automatic-Stay Provision

• • •

ANYONE WHO HAS DEALT WITH ECMC as a debtor knows that it is a heartless organization. As one of the federal government's student-loan debt collectors, it has harassed hapless creditors thousands of times. It was ECMC that opposed bankruptcy relief for Janet Roth, an elderly woman with chronic health problems who was living on less than $800 a month.

But the *Roth* case does not fully display ECMC's callousness. A better illustration of its merciless behavior is found in *Bruner-Halteman v. ECMC*, which was decided by a Texas bankruptcy court in April 2016.[1]

Bruner-Halteman was a single mother who worked at Starbucks, living, as the bankruptcy court observed, "on the ragged edge where any adversity can be catastrophic."[2] She owed about $5,000 on a student loan issued by Sallie Mae, and she was in default.

In 2012, ECMC garnished Bruner-Halteman's Starbucks wages, and she filed for bankruptcy, which, under federal law, triggers

1 Bruner-Halteman v. Educational Credit Management Corp., Case No. 12-324-HDH-13, ADV. No. 14-03041 (Bankr. N.D. Tex. 2016).
2 Ibid., *4.

an automatic stay of all garnishment activities. ECMC received notice of the bankruptcy filing and even participated as a creditor in Bruner-Halteman's bankruptcy proceedings. But it continued to garnish Bruner-Halteman's wages for almost two years.

In fact, ECMC garnished Bruner-Halteman's wages thirty-seven times *after* she filed for bankruptcy—a clear violation of federal law. Moreover, ECMC had no reasonable excuse for its misbehavior. In fact, ECMC refunded the wages it garnished on seventeen occasions but kept on garnishing this poor woman's wages. Indeed, the garnishments did not stop until Bruner-Halteman filed a lawsuit for damages in the bankruptcy court.

The bankruptcy court held a three-day trial on Bruner-Halteman's claims and heard plenty of evidence about the stress Bruner-Halteman experienced due to ECMC's illegal garnishments. On April 8, 2016, the court awarded her actual damages of about $8,000, attorney fees, and $74,000 in punitive damages.

Here is how the bankruptcy judge summarized ECMC's conduct: "ECMC's systematic, knowing, and willful disregard of the automatic stay and the protections afforded a debtor by the bankruptcy system was particularly egregious and offends the integrity of the bankruptcy process...The indifference shown by ECMC to the Plaintiff and the bankruptcy process is gravely disturbing."[3]

The court was particularly offended by the fact that ECMC repeatedly refunded the amounts it garnished but did not stop the garnishment process. "The callousness of the refund process is particularly rattling," the court wrote.[4]

"In order to process a refund," the court noted, "an ECMC employee had to make the determination that the debtor had an active bankruptcy case, but that did nothing to convince ECMC that it should be cancelling the wage garnishments." Instead, ECMC

---

3 Ibid., *8.
4 Ibid, *9.

processed the refunds "at whatever pace it chose" while Bruner-Halteman "was doing everything she could to make ends meet." [5]

At the conclusion of its opinion, the court summarized ECMC's behavior as follows: "A sophisticated creditor, ECMC, active in many cases in this district and across the country, decided that it could continue to garnish a debtor's wages with full knowledge that she was in a pending bankruptcy case. The Plaintiff, a woman who suffers from a severe medical condition, was hurt in the process. She was deprived of the full use of her paycheck. She incurred significant attorneys' fees in trying to fix the situation. A garnishment of a few hundred dollars may not be much to everyone, but to Kristin Bruner-Halteman, it meant a lot."[6]

I will make just two comments about ECMC's merciless and cruel behavior in the *Bruner-Halteman* case. First, $74,000 might be a significant punitive-damages award for some organizations, but it is peanuts to ECMC. After all, the Century Foundation reported recently that ECMC, a nonprofit organization, has $1 billion in cash and unrestricted assets.[7] A punitive damages award of a million dollars would have been more appropriate.

Second, Ms. Bruner-Halteman was not awarded damages for ECMC's outlaw conduct until April 8, 2016, almost exactly four years after ECMC's first wrongful garnishment. Obviously, ECMC knows how to stretch out the litigation process to wear down its adversaries.

ECMC's name has appeared as a named party in hundreds of court decisions. A little dust-up like the one it had with Bruner-Halteman is simply the price of doing business in the dirty commerce of harassing student-loan defaulters. And you can bet no one

---

5 Ibid.

6 Ibid.

7 Robert Shireman and Tariq Habash, *Have Student Loan Guaranty Agencies Lost Their Way?* (The Century Foundation: September 29, 2016), accessed August, 5, 2017, https://tcf.org/content/report/student-loan-guaranty-agencies-lost-way/.

at ECMC missed a meal or lost any sleep because of the *Bruner-Halteman* case.

Perhaps some US senators who publicly bemoan the excesses of the student-loan industry should hold Senate hearings and ask ECMC's CEO a few questions, such as the following: How much do ECMC executives pay themselves? How did ECMC accumulate $1 billion in unrestricted assets? And who is paying ECMC's attorney fees for hounding all those American student-loan borrowers—millions of whom, like Bruner-Halteman, are living "on the ragged edge"?

Sara Fern v. FedLoan Servicing: A Single Mother of Three Discharges Her Student Loans in Bankruptcy over the Objections of the US Department of Education

• • •

Student loans cannot be discharged in bankruptcy, right? *Wrong!* Distressed student borrowers have won a string of victories in the bankruptcy courts over the past few years. And *Fern v. FedLoan Servicing* is another case for the win column.

In 2016, Sara Fern, a thirty-five-year-old mother of three children, discharged about $27,000 in student loans in an Iowa bankruptcy court.[1] And in February 2017, her victory was affirmed by the Bankruptcy Appellate Panel of the Eighth Circuit Court of Appeals.[2]

Between 2002 and 2007, Fern borrowed approximately $20,000 to pay for courses in vocational programs. Over the years, Fern had not made a single payment on her student loans, and by the time of her bankruptcy trial (her adversary proceeding), Fern's accumulated debt totaled about $27,000. Nevertheless, she had never been in default because her loans had always been in deferment or forbearance due to her economic circumstances.

At the time of her bankruptcy trial, Fern was a single mother of three children, subsisting on take-home pay of $1,506.78 a month In addition, she received $368 a month in food stamps and public rental

---

1 Fern v. Fedloan Servicing, 553 B.R. 362 (Bankr. N.D. Iowa 2016), *aff'd*, 563 B. R. 1 (B.A.P. 8th Cir. 2017).

2 Fern v. FedLoan Servicing, 563 B. R. 1 (B.A.P. 8th Cir. 2017).

assistance valued at $538. Fern drove an old car in need of repair, and she could not afford to buy a more reliable vehicle.

Although Fern attempted to improve her income status by taking out student loans to enroll in two postsecondary programs, neither program led to a higher-paying job. As the bankruptcy court noted, Fern had never earned more than $25,000 a year.

The DOE opposed Fern's effort to shed her student loans in bankruptcy. The DOE produced an expert witness who testified that Fern qualified for various IBRPs. According to the expert, Fern's income was so low that her monthly payments would be zero if she entered one of these plans.

But Judge Thad Collins, an Iowa bankruptcy judge, rejected the DOE's arguments and discharged Fern's student loans in their entirety. In Judge Collins's view, Fern would probably never be in a financial position to pay back her loans.

Under an IBRP, Judge Collins noted, Fern's monthly payments would be zero, but her debt would continue to grow as interest accrued on the unpaid balance. Although the government would forgive any unpaid portion of Fern's loans at the end of the repayment period (twenty or twenty-five years in the future), the cancelled debt might be taxable to her. In addition, if Fern's student loans were not discharged, they would be a blot on her credit record.

Judge Collins Recognizes Emotional Stress from Long-Term Indebtedness

Judge Collins also considered the emotional distress that comes from long-term indebtedness; Fern's loans had already caused her emotional stress, Collins observed, and she would continue to suffer from emotional stress if she were forced into a long-term repayment plan: "This mounting indebtedness has also indisputably been an emotional burden on [Fern]. [She] testified that knowing that the debt is hanging over her, constantly growing, and that she will never be able to repay this debt, is distressing to her. [Fern] testified that she feels like she will never be able to get ahead because she will always have this debt."[3]

In Judge Collins's opinion, the emotional burden of long-term indebtedness was a hardship that weighed in favor of discharging Fern's student loans, even though this burden could not be quantified. "The Court will not ignore a hardship," Collins wrote, "simply because it is not reflected on a balance sheet."[4]

The Department of Education Appeals Judge Collins's Decision

The DOE appealed Judge Collins's decision, and in February 2017, the Bankruptcy Appellate Panel of the Eighth Circuit Court of Appeals affirmed Collins's ruling. At the appellate level, the DOE argued that Judge Collins erred by taking Fern's emotional burdens into account, by considering the tax consequences of a long-term repayment plan, and by recognizing that Fern's debt would grow over the years because her monthly payments under a long-term plan (zero), would cause interest on her loans to continue accumulating.

But the Eighth Circuit's Bankruptcy Appellate Panel disagreed. "These additional observations identified by the Bankruptcy Court simply served to supplement its determination of undue hardship under the totality of circumstances test," the B.A.P. court wrote.[5]

The *Fern* decision is a big win for student-loan debtors. This is the latest federal appellate court decision to reject creditors' arguments

---

3 Fern v. FedLoan Servicing, 553 B.R. at 370.
4 Ibid.
5 Fern v. FedLoan Servicing, 563 B.R. at 5.

that bankrupt student borrowers should be pushed into twenty- or twenty-five-year repayment plans instead of getting a fresh start.

THERE IS JUSTICE IN THE WORLD (SOMETIMES)

As one of Cormac McCarthy's fictional characters said in the novel, *The Crossing,* "*Quizás hay poca de justicia en este mundo.*"[6] (Perhaps there is little justice in this world.)

But there is *some* justice in the world, although it is distributed unevenly and sometimes arrives too late to do us any good. Sara Fern was very fortunate to have obtained justice from Judge Thad Collins, who wrote a remarkably sensible and compassionate decision. And she was even more fortunate to have Judge Collins's decision affirmed on appeal by the Eighth Circuit's Bankruptcy Appellate Panel.

---

6 Cormac McCarthy, *The Crossing* (New York: Alfred A Knopf, 1994), 293.

Murray v. Educational Credit Management Corporation: A Kansas Bankruptcy Court Discharged All the Accrued Interest on a Married Couple's Student Loans

• • •

DO YOU REMEMBER POLITICAL CONSULTANT James Carville's famous line during the 1992 presidential campaign? "It's the economy, stupid," Carville supposedly observed.[1] That eloquently simple remark became Bill Clinton's distilled campaign message and helped propel him into the presidency.

Something similar might be said about the student-loan crisis: "It's the interest, stupid." In fact, for many Americans, it is the interest and penalties on their student loans—not the amount they borrowed—which are causing them so much financial distress.

THE REMARKABLE CASE OF MURRAY V. EDUCATIONAL CREDIT MANAGEMENT CORPORATION

This truth is starkly illustrated in the case of *Murray v. Educational Credit Management Corporation*, which was decided by a Kansas

---

1 Jerry Jasinowski, "It's the Economy, Stupid," *Huffpost* (blog), November 5, 2015, accessed August 6, 2017, http://www.huffingtonpost.com/jerry-jasinowski/presidential-debates_b_8478456.html.

bankruptcy judge in December 2016.[2] At the time they filed for bankruptcy, Alan and Catherine Murray owed $311,000 in student-loan debt, even though they had only borrowed about $77,000. Thus, 75 percent of their total debt represented interest on their loans, which had accrued over almost twenty years at an annual rate of 9 percent.

As Judge Dale Somers explained in his ruling on the case, the Murrays had taken out thirty-one student loans back in the 1990s to obtain bachelor's degrees and master's degrees. In 1996, when they consolidated their loans, they only owed a total of $77,524.

Over the years, the Murrays made loan payments when they could, which totaled $54,000—more than half the amount they borrowed.[3] Nevertheless, they entered into several forbearance agreements that allowed them to skip payments, and they also signed up for IDRs that reduced the amounts of their monthly payments. Meanwhile, interest on their debt continued to accrue. By the time the Murrays filed for bankruptcy in 2014, their $77,000 debt had grown to almost a third of a million dollars.

The Murrays' combined income was substantial—about $95,000. Educational Credit Management Corporation (ECMC), the creditor in the case, argued that the Murrays had enough discretionary income to make significant loan payments in an IDR. In fact, under such a plan, their monthly loan payments would be less than $1,000 a month,

But Judge Somers disagreed. Interest on the Murrays' debt was accruing at the rate of $65 a day, Judge Somers pointed out—about $2,000 a month.[4] Clearly, the couple would never pay off their loan under ECMC's proposed repayment plan. Instead, their debt would grow larger with each passing month.

---

2 Murray v. Educational Credit Management Corp., 563 B.R. 52(Bankr. D. Kan. 2016).

3 Ibid., 55.

4 Ibid., 57.

On the other hand, in Judge Somers's view, the Murrays had sufficient income to pay off the principle of their loan and still maintain a minimal standard of living. Thus, he crafted a remarkably sensible ruling whereby the interest on the Murrays' debt was discharged but not the principle. The Murrays are still obligated to pay the $77,000 they borrowed back in the 1990s plus future interest on this amount, which would begin accruing at the rate of 9 percent commencing on the date of the court's judgment.[5]

JUDGE SOMERS POINTS THE WAY TO SENSIBLE STUDENT-DEBT RELIEF

In my view, Judge Somers's decision in the *Murray* case is a sensible way to address the student-debt crisis. Eight million people have defaulted on their loans, and another 5 million are making token payments under IDRs that are often not large enough to cover the accruing interest. Millions of Americans have obtained loan deferments that allow them to skip their loan payments, but these people—like the Murrays—are seeing their loan balances grow each month as interest accrues.

Judge Somers's decision doesn't solve the student-loan crisis in its entirety, but it is a good solution for millions of people whose loan balances have doubled, tripled, and even quadrupled due to accrued interest amounts, penalties, and fees.

Obviously, Judge Somers's solution should only be offered to people who dealt with their loans in good faith. Judge Somers specifically ruled that the Murrays had acted in good faith regarding their loans. In fact, they paid back about 70 percent of the amount they borrowed.

---

5 Ibid., 62.

Unfortunately, but not surprisingly, ECMC appealed the *Murray* decision, hoping to overturn it. As of this writing, an appellate ruling has not been issued. Nevertheless, let us take heart from the fact that a Kansas bankruptcy judge reviewed a married couple's financial disaster and crafted a fair and humane solution.

Morgan v. Sanford Brown Institute: New Jersey Supreme Court Strikes Down an Arbitration Clause in Sanford Brown Institute's Student-Enrollment Agreements: Another Nail in the Coffin for the For-Profit College Industry

• • •

ALMOST ALL FOR-PROFIT COLLEGES REQUIRE their students to sign arbitration agreements as a condition of enrollment. In essence, students who sign arbitration agreements give up their rights to sue the college they attend, even if they believe they have been victims of fraud or deceptive business practices.

Why do the for-profit colleges insist that students arbitrate their grievances instead of filing lawsuits? There are several reasons.

First, most commentators agree that arbitration generally favors a corporate entity over a private party. Arbitrators make good money settling disputes, and they know they are likely to have future dealings with corporations such as for-profit colleges. Arbitrators do not want to get a reputation for being hard on for-profit colleges because they know the for-profits will not choose them to arbitrate future disputes. Thus, their rulings may be more likely to favor a for-profit college over a humble student or at least may limit the amounts of damages that might get awarded against a college engaged in wrongdoing.

Second, arbitration usually takes place in a private setting, and arbitrators' decisions are generally not made public. If a for-profit college loses an arbitration case, other potential plaintiffs are not likely to find out about it.

Finally, arbitration clauses generally preclude students from banding together and bringing class-action suits against allegedly deceitful colleges, and these clauses often require student grievants to bring their arbitration disputes in a jurisdiction that favors the college.

Under the Obama administration, the DOE signaled that it disfavored the for-profits colleges' practice of forcing students to give up their rights to sue as a condition of enrollment, and it drafted regulations that would ban this practice.[1] But these regulations were put on hold by President Trump's Secretary of Education, Betsy DeVos in June 2017.[2] Thus, as of the summer of 2017, for profit colleges may still require their students to sign mandatory arbitration agreements as a condition of enrollment.

But the courts may be changing their views. Recently, a California appellate court invalidated an arbitration clause signed by California students who had enrolled in a nursing program with an Indiana education provider.[3]

And in June 2016, in the case of *Morgan v. Sanford Brown Institute*, the New Jersey Supreme Court invalidated an arbitration clause that Sanford Brown Institute required students to sign. The students had

---

1 "US Department of Education Takes Further Steps to Protect Students from Predatory Higher Education Institutions," March 11, 2016, accessed August 5, 2017, http://www.ed.gov/news/press-releases/us-department-education-takes-further-steps-protect-students-predatory-higher-education-institutions?

2 Andrew Kreighbaum, "Few Solutions for Defrauded Borrowers," *Inside Higher Ed*, June 26, 2017, accessed August 6, 2017, https://www.insidehighered.com/news/2017/06/26/advocates-say-department-inaction-forced-arbitration-leave-defrauded-borrowers-bind.

3 Magno v. The College Network, Inc., 204 Cal. Rptr. 3d 829 (Cal. Ct. App. 2016).

enrolled in an ultrasound-technician program, and they accused Sanford Brown of engaging in deceptive practices.[4]

Specifically, the students alleged that Sanford Brown had "misrepresented the value of the school's ultrasound technician program and the quality of its instructors, instructed students on outdated equipment and with inadequate teaching materials, provided insufficient career-service counseling, and conveyed inaccurate information about Sanford Brown's accreditation status."[5] The students also claimed that Sanford Brown had "employed high-pressure and deceptive business tactics that resulted in plaintiffs financing their education with high-interest loans, passing up the study of ultrasound at a reputable college, and losing career advancement opportunities."[6]

Sanford Brown asked a New Jersey court to force the students to arbitrate their claims pursuant to the arbitration clause in the students' enrollment agreements. That clause, according to the New Jersey Supreme Court, consisted of "thirty-five unbroken lines of nine-point Times New Roman font,"[7] including this murky passage:

> *Agreement to Arbitrate*—Any disputes, claims, or controversies between the parties to this Enrollment Agreement arising out of or relating to (i) this Enrollment Agreement; (ii) the Student's recruitment, enrollment, attendance, or education; (iii) financial aid or career service assistance by SBI; (iv) any claim, no matter how described, pleaded or styled, relating in any manner, to any act or omission regarding the Student's relationship with SBI, its employees, or with externship sites or their employees; or (v) any objection to arbitrability or the existence, scope, validity, construction, or enforceability of

---

4 Morgan v. Sanford Brown Institute, 137 A.3d 1168 (N. J. 2016).
5 Ibid., 1172-73.
6 Ibid., 1173.
7 Ibid.

this Arbitration Agreement shall be resolved pursuant to this paragraph.[8]

Ultimately, the New Jersey Supreme Court ruled in the case, and the court invalidated Sanford Brown's arbitration clause. In the court's view, the clause was not "written in plain language that would be clear and understandable to the average consumer that she is giving up the right to pursue relief in a judicial forum."[9] (I have omitted internal quotation marks and citations for greater clarity here.)

"In summary," the court concluded, "the arbitration provision and purported delegation clause in Sanford Brown's enrollment agreement failed to explain in some sufficiently broad way or otherwise that that arbitration was a substitute for having disputes and legal claims resolved before a judge or jury."[10] Without some minimal knowledge of the meaning of arbitration, the court ruled, the complaining students could not give informed assent to arbitration and to waiving their right to seek relief in a court.

The New Jersey Supreme Court's *Morgan* decision is a good decision for all students who have been wronged by a for-profit college. Following on the heels of a similar decision in California, the *Morgan* opinion drives another nail into the coffin of the for-profit college industry, which has protected itself from liability for deceptive and fraudulent practices by forcing its students to waive their rights to sue. In New Jersey and California at least, students now have a better chance of getting their claims against allegedly deceptive for-profit colleges heard by a court. And if students are successful in their cases and obtain substantial judgments against the colleges that wronged them, some of these colleges will be forced to close.

And that, in my opinion, would be a good development.

---

8 Ibid., 1173-74.
9 Ibid., 1181.
10 Ibid., 1182.

Conner v. US Department of Education: Middle-Aged People Should Probably Not Go to Graduate School

• • •

WAGES FOR AMERICAN WORKERS HAVE been stagnant for more than twenty years; everyone knows that. In fact, many American workers have seen a decline in their real wages as inflation eats away at their paychecks.

A college degree supposedly enhances earnings, but not for everyone. More than a third of college-educated workers are holding jobs that do not require a college degree.

As we drift into middle age, we search for ways to make more money. So why not go to graduate school? Maybe job opportunities will open up if we get an MBA. Or maybe we can unleash our creative capacity if we obtain a master's degree in creative writing. Why not go to law school?

Of course, American colleges want people to think that going to graduate school is a good career option. Undergraduate enrollments are declining at many universities—especially at the second-tier liberal-arts schools. The colleges have got to keep the money flowing, and many have been rolling out new graduate programs to enhance their revenues. Juicing up MBA programs has been a favorite strategy.

Graduate programs can be expensive, and most people who pursue graduate degrees have to take out student loans to finance their studies. But, hey—what could go wrong? There are at least three things.

Age Discrimination

Although federal laws protect people from age discrimination in the workplace, many employers discriminate against older workers. So if you are forty-five years old and recently obtained a law degree or an MBA, you will be competing against much younger workers.

Law firms in particular are looking for bright *young* attorneys who have the drive and energy to work eighty hours a week. The firms like to mold their new hires into their corporate cultures, and it is easier to mold a twenty-five-year old than a forty-five-year old. And the firms definitely discriminate in favor of people who graduated from top-ranked law schools.

So if you graduated from a second- or third-tier law school at age forty-five, the chances of landing a high-paying job at a blue-chip law firm are virtually zero. And if you borrowed $140,000 to get your law degree (the average amount of debt for new law graduates), you are in real trouble. In fact, your decision to borrow money to go to law school was probably a mistake.

Many Graduate Programs Don't Give Students Useful Skills

Second, a lot of graduate programs do not teach skills that will enhance their students' marketability in the workplace. The United States now has hundreds of MBA programs, but I have talked with people who got MBA degrees from nonelite colleges, and several told me they didn't learn much.

I myself was a sucker. I enrolled in the doctoral program at the Harvard Graduate School of Education, thinking a doctorate in education policy from Harvard would open doors for me that I couldn't open with just my law degree. In fact, I learned virtually nothing useful during my two years of study at Harvard other than the fact that the school is a pretty mediocre place.

Unsympathetic Bankruptcy Courts

Several recent bankruptcy court decisions have involved middle-aged people who accumulated a lot of debt going to graduate school. Some of these people argued that their advanced ages should be considered—that they simply didn't have enough working years left to pay off their enormous student-loan debts.

But not all bankruptcy courts are sympathetic. In *Conner v. US Department of Education*, for example, Patricia Monet Conner accumulated $214,000 in student-loan debt to pay for graduate education in three fields: business administration, communications, and education.[1]

Conner was a schoolteacher who had an annual income of about $60,000 during the years before she filed bankruptcy, and she never made a single voluntary payment on her student loans. When she came before the bankruptcy court, Conner was sixty-one years old, and she argued that her advanced age should be considered in her favor.

But the bankruptcy court rejected Conner's argument and refused to discharge her student-loan debt. Conner appealed, and a federal district court was equally unsympathetic. "Courts have regularly held that one's age cannot form the bases of a favorable finding for a debtor who chooses to pursue an education later in life," the court ruled.[2]

---

1 Conner v. US Department of Education, Case No. 15-1-541, 2016 WL 1178264 (E. D. Mich. March 28, 2016).
2 Ibid., *3.

CONCLUSION: MIDDLE-AGED PEOPLE SHOULD BE VERY CAUTIOUS ABOUT GOING TO GRADUATE SCHOOL

Many Americans enter middle age without having achieved the goals they set for themselves when they were young. I myself am such a person. Going to graduate school may seem like a way to expand life's opportunities—a second chance to obtain success.

But be very cautious. Gamblers who lose at the gaming tables often double down, hoping a big win will nullify their earlier losses. But unlucky gamblers who keep betting generally wind up losing more money. Universities, like casinos, want you to think the odds are in your favor, but in fact they are not.

I do not give this advice out of a sense of superiority. As I said, I made a big mistake going to Harvard in midlife only to find that some of my professors were not as smart as I am. I wound up with a mediocre education and a lot of debt.

Sandy Baum's New Book on Student Debt Contains Some Good Ideas

• • •

SOME PUBLIC POLICY COMMENTATORS DRASTICALLY understate the enormity of the student-loan crisis. But Sandy Baum's new book, *Student Debt: Rhetoric and Realities of Higher Education Financing*, contains some good ideas, which I endorse.[1] Here are some of her most important recommendations.

DON'T GARNISH SOCIAL SECURITY PAYMENTS

I have long argued that the federal government should stop garnishing the Social Security checks of elderly student-loan defaulters. Baum agrees. As she put it, it is one thing for the government to garnish wages of student-loan defaulters or scoop up defaulters' tax refunds, but "further diminishing the living standards of senior citizens...with no potential for labor market earnings who are struggling to make ends meet on their Social Security payments is quite another thing."[2] Bravo.

---

1 Sandy Baum, *Student Debt: Rhetoric and Realities of Higher Education Financing* (New York: Palgrave-MacMillan, 2016).
2 Ibid., 97.

STOP GIVING PRIVATE LENDERS SPECIAL PROTECTION IN THE BANKRUPTCY COURTS

In 2005, Congress amended the Bankruptcy Code to make private student loans nondischargeable in bankruptcy unless the borrower could show undue hardship, which is the same standard that applies to federal student loans. This is wrong.

As Baum observed, "there is no good reason for the government to sanction these unsecured loans as student loans or to grant them any special provisions, particularly...protection from bankruptcy proceedings."[3] This is an eminently sensible observation, and other respected policy commentators agree with Baum on this.

TREAT STUDENT LOANS LIKE ANY OTHER UNSECURED DEBT IN BANKRUPTCY

I have argued for years that student loans should be treated like any other unsecured debt in bankruptcy and that the undue-hardship provision in the bankruptcy code should be repealed or at least interpreted far more humanely.

I was heartened to read that Baum, a leading expert on the federal student-loan program, agrees with me on this point. Indeed, reforming bankruptcy laws to allow distressed student-loan debtors relief from oppressive student-loan debt is the key to reforming the entire student-loan program.

BAUM PROPOSES OTHER REFORMS AS WELL

Baum made some other good points in her book. For example, some limits should be placed on the amount of money people can borrow to fund their college studies, and some limit needs to be placed on the amount of interest that can accrue on student-loan debt. She also

---

3 Ibid., 97-98.

said limits should be placed on the amount elderly people can borrow to fund their studies since they won't work long enough to pay off enormous amounts of student-loan debt.

Baum's book covers other topics as well, but the reforms I've listed here are critical. If the policy makers aren't going to listen to me (and so far they have not), then perhaps they will listen to Sandy Baum.

Let Justice Roll On like a River: Richard Precht, a Virginia Man Living on $1,200 a Month, Won Bankruptcy Discharge of Nearly $100,000 in Student-Loan Debt

● ● ●

But let justice roll on like a river, righteousness
like a never-failing stream!

—AMOS 5:24

ON JULY 7, 2015, THE DOE issued a letter outlining guidelines for determining when the Department and its student-loan collection agencies would not oppose bankruptcy relief for distressed student-loan debtors. The DOE listed eleven factors that it would consider, including these:

1. "Whether a debtor is approaching retirement, taking into account the debtor's age at the time student loans were incurred and resources likely to be available to the debtor in retirement to repay a student loan..."
2. "Whether a debtor's health has materially changed since the student loan debt was incurred..."[1]

_____

1 Letter from Lynn Mahaffie, Deputy Assistant Secretary for Policy, Planning and Innovation, "Undue Hardship Discharge of Title IV Loans in Bankruptcy

Frankly, I thought the DOE's letter was insincere, that the DOE would continue to oppose bankruptcy relief for nearly everyone, and that it would persist in insisting that virtually every distressed student-loan debtor must be placed in a long-term IBRP. But perhaps I was wrong.

In October 2015, Richard Precht, age sixty-eight, filed for bankruptcy and asked to have his student-loan debt discharged. Mr. Precht, as it turned out, was the perfect person to test whether the DOE meant what it said in its July 2015 letter. He was living in retirement and was in ill health and was burdened with almost $100,000 in student-loan debt.

In fact, his circumstances were desperate. Mr. Precht was living on a small pension and a small Social Security check, but both were being garnished by the federal government. His total income was only $1,200 a month, and he was forced to live with his adult daughter because his income was not sufficient for him to afford housing.

Precht filed for bankruptcy in Virginia, and the federal court system quickly issued a scheduling order that put his case on track for a trial before a bankruptcy judge. Fortunately, Mr. Precht was ready to proceed with his case without delay. He had prepared nearly a thousand pages of exhibits outlining his financial circumstances, his health status, and his loan-payment history over the years.

Initially, the DOE opposed Precht's petition for relief. The DOE's lawyer filed a motion to strike, asking the bankruptcy judge to order Precht to refile his complaint on technical grounds. But fortunately for Mr. Precht, the bankruptcy judge had read the DOE's July 2015 letter.

At the hearing, the judge pointedly asked the DOE's attorney what the DOE planned to do about that letter. The attorney's candid reply was, "We don't know."

Adversary Proceedings," DCL ID: Gen-15-13, July 7, 2017, accessed August 3, 2017, https://ifap.ed.gov/dpcletters/attachments/GEN1513.pdf.

But apparently, the policy makers at the DOE considered the matter and decided to do the right thing. A few days after the hearing on the DOE's motion to strike, the DOE attorney called Mr. Precht and said the Department would not oppose bankruptcy relief. The DOE prepared an order for the bankruptcy judge to sign that relieved Mr. Precht of all his bankruptcy debt—a miracle of almost biblical proportions.[2]

As the prophet Amos said: "Let justice roll on like a river."[3] Mr. Precht won a life-altering victory for himself, and his case points the way for hundreds of thousands of people who are similarly situated. More than 150,000 elderly student-loan debtors are having their Social Security checks garnished, and millions of people are now in long-term IBRPs that obligate them to pay on their student-loans until they are in their seventies, their eighties, and even their nineties.

Personally, I don't think Mr. Precht's victory signals a change of attitude at the DOE. I think he was able to prevail because he was prepared to go to trial and his case was so strong. As of this writing, the DOE still opposes bankruptcy relief for almost all student borrowers.

Nevertheless, Mr. Precht's victory is significant. His case demonstrates that truly deserving student-loan debtors who prepare good cases can prevail in bankruptcy court, even if they are not represented by attorneys.

---

2 Precht v. US Department of Education, AD PRO 15-01167-RGM (Bankr. E.D. Va. Feb. 11, 2016)(Consent Order).

3 Amos 5:24.

Discharging Student Loans in Bankruptcy: A Field Guide for People Who Have Nothing to Lose

● ● ●

STUDENT LOANS CANNOT BE DISCHARGED in bankruptcy. How often have you heard that said? But that bromide is not true. Student loans are being discharged—or at least partly discharged—in the bankruptcy courts every year.

So if you are a distressed student borrower who will never pay back your student loans, why not attempt to discharge your college loans through bankruptcy? What have you got to lose?

You say you don't have the money to pay a lawyer to represent you in bankruptcy court. Then represent yourself. Again—what have you got to lose?

This essay is a field guide for struggling debtors who are thinking about filing for bankruptcy to discharge their student loans. This is a difficult process, and not everyone will be successful. In fact, much depends upon drawing a sympathetic bankruptcy judge. But you will not know whether your college debt is dischargeable through bankruptcy unless you make the effort. So let's get started.

DISCHARGING STUDENT LOANS IN BANKRUPTCY: THE UNDUE HARDSHIP RULE
Section 523(a)(8) of the Bankruptcy Code states that a student loan cannot be discharged in bankruptcy unless the debtor can show that

paying the loan would pose an undue hardship on the debtor and his or her dependents.

Congress did not define *undue hardship* when it adopted this provision, so it has been left to the courts to define. Most federal circuits have adopted the *Brunner* test, named for a 1987 federal court decision.[1] The *Brunner* test contains three parts:

1. Debtors cannot maintain, based on current income and expenses, a minimal standard of living for themselves and their dependents if forced to repay the loans.
2. Additional circumstances exist indicating that this state of affairs is likely to persist for a significant portion of the repayment period of the student loans.
3. Debtors have made good-faith efforts to repay the loans.

Although most bankruptcy courts and federal appellate courts utilize the *Brunner* test when deciding student-loan bankruptcy cases, there are remarkable variations among the courts about how the *Brunner* test is interpreted, with some courts interpreting it more favorably for debtors than others.

FILING AN ADVERSARY COMPLAINT

Filing for bankruptcy is a relatively straightforward process—particularly for people who have no assets. Many lawyers will walk you through a Chapter 7 bankruptcy for a flat fee.

But discharging your federal student loans requires you to file an adversary action—a separate lawsuit—against your student-loan creditors, which may be the US DOE, a student-loan guaranty agency, or one of the government's approved debt collectors. And

---

1 Brunner v. New York State Higher Education Services Corporation, 831 F.2d 395, 396 (2d Cir. 1987).

if you have private student loans, you will need to sue your private creditor as well.

Drafting a complaint for your adversary action is not difficult; you can find forms on the web or in published bankruptcy guides.

GATHERING YOUR EVIDENCE BEFORE YOU FILE YOUR ADVERSARY COMPLAINT

In my view, you should gather all your documentary evidence before you file your adversary complaint. That evidence should include:

1. All the records you have of payments that you made
2. Correspondence with your creditor
3. Documents supporting efforts you made to find employment
4. Evidence of health problems, disability status, and any other documents that support your claim that paying off your student loans would be an undue hardship

In addition, if you negotiated with your creditor about entering into a long-term IBRP, gather the documents that show what efforts you made to explore repayment options.

If relevant, you should also gather evidence showing that the job market for your profession is bad. People who attended law school, for example, should provide evidence of the bad job market for newly graduated lawyers. If you failed the bar exam or another pertinent licensing exam, you should gather evidence establishing that fact.

If you attended a for-profit school that has been found guilty of fraud or misrepresentation, you should obtain documents to educate the bankruptcy judge about your school's misbehavior.

Why is it important to gather your evidence before you file your adversary complaint? There are two reasons. One of the first things your creditor will do after you file your lawsuit is send you discovery requests:

1. Interrogatories (questions) about your financial status and your expenses
2. Requests for production of your documents
3. Requests for admissions

Having your documents prepared in advance will enable you to respond to your creditor's requests for documents in a timely manner and will subtly communicate that you are prepared to have your case go to trial.

Secondly, assembling your documents early will help you determine the strengths and weaknesses of your case before you file your adversary complaint. For example, if you are disabled or have medical problems, evidence about your health status will be helpful in establishing undue hardship.

On the other hand, if you made few or no payments on your student loans over the years, that is a negative fact for you because the creditor will argue that you did not manage your loans in good faith. Courts have discharged student loans in several cases in which the student debtor made no voluntary loan payments, but you will want to be able to argue that you meet the good-faith test in spite of your spotty payment history.

KNOWING THE CASE LAW ABOUT STUDENT LOANS AND BANKRUPTCY IN YOUR JURISDICTION

It is also important that you know how courts have ruled in student-loan cases in your jurisdiction. If you live within the boundaries of the Ninth Circuit, you will want to be familiar with the decisions in the *Roth*, *Hedlund*, *Scott*, and *Nys* cases.[2] If you live in the Tenth

---

2 Roth v. Educational Management Corporation., 490 B. R. 908 (B.A.P. 9th Cir. 2013); Hedlund v. Educational Resources Institute, Inc. and Pennsylvania Higher Education Assistance Agency, 718 F.3d 848 (9th Cir. 2013); Scott v. US

Circuit, you will want to know about the *Polleys* decision.[3] If you are in the Seventh Circuit, the *Krieger* decision is important to you.[4]

BEING PSYCHOLOGICALLY PREPARED FOR A LONG COURT BATTLE

Published court decisions show that the DOE and the student-loan guaranty agencies are sometimes willing to fight student debtors in the courts for a long time. In the *Hedlund* case, for example, involving a law graduate who failed to pass the bar exam, the creditor fought Mr. Hedlund in the federal courts for ten years.[5]

Why do the student-loan creditors drag out litigation with bankrupt student borrowers? There are three reasons: First, the student-loan guaranty agencies are well funded, and they can afford to pay attorney fees in a particular case, even if the case drags on for years. And of course, the DOE has free government attorneys to represent its interests.

Second, by filing appeals and driving up litigation costs, the DOE and the student-loan guaranty agencies know they are demoralizing student debtors, making it more likely they will abandon their lawsuits. Even debtors who prevail in the bankruptcy court without having a lawyer find it daunting to participate in the appellate process without an attorney to represent them.

And third, by imposing heavy financial and psychological costs on people who file adversary actions, the DOE knows that it is

---

Department of Education, 417 B. R. 623 (Bankr. W. D. Wash. 2009); Educational Credit Management Corporation v. Nys, 446 F.3d 938 (9th Cir. 2006).

3 Educational Credit Management Corporation v. Polleys, 356 F.3d 1302 (10th Cir. 2004).

4 Krieger v. Educational Credit Management Corporation, 713 F.3d 882 (7th Cir. 2013).

5 Hedlund v. The Educational Resources Institute, Inc. and Pennsylvania. Higher Educ. Assistance Agency, 718 F.3d 848 (9th Cir. 2013).

discouraging distressed debtors from even trying to discharge their student loans in bankruptcy.

BEING APPROPRIATELY SUSPICIOUS OF ANY DOCUMENT A CREDITOR'S ATTORNEY ASKS YOU TO SIGN

Once you file your lawsuit, be aware of two potential dangers. First, the DOE or one of its debt collectors will probably send you a request for admissions. Do not ignore that document. If you fail to respond to a request for admissions, the statement you are asked to admit is deemed admitted. It is very important to remember that.

Second, it is improper for a party to ask an opposing party to admit a principle of law. For example, it would be improper for a request for admission to ask you to admit that it would not be an undue hardship for you to repay your student loans.

Obviously, you should answer all interrogatories and requests for admissions truthfully, but do not admit to propositions that you are unclear about or which you do not understand. If you do not know the answer to a question, it is permissible to state that you do not know.

Similarly, don't sign a stipulation of facts that a creditor's attorneys asks you to sign unless you are very clear that signing a stipulation won't prejudice your case in court. And remember—when a government attorney waves a stipulation in your face and asks you to sign it, the attorney is not making that request to help you. The lawyer drafted that stipulation to help the government.

WINNING YOUR ADVERSARY ACTION AND THE CREDITOR APPEALS

In several instances, student-loan debtors have gone to court without attorneys and won their cases. It has been my observation that some bankruptcy judges are sympathetic to people who are overwhelmed by student-loan debt, and these judges have written remarkably thorough decisions ruling in the debtor's favor.

But sometimes the creditor appeals, forcing the debtor to figure out how to file a strong appellate brief. For example, Alexandra Acosta-Conniff won a student-loan discharge in an Alabama bankruptcy court without being represented by a lawyer,[6] and George and Melanie Johnson won their case before a Kansas bankruptcy judge, even though they filed their adversary proceeding without an attorney.[7] In both cases, the debtors were opposed by ECMC, and in both cases, ECMC appealed.

In my view, debtors need attorneys to represent them in appellate proceedings, so debtors who win their cases at the bankruptcy-court level without lawyers need to find appellate lawyers to help them if their bankruptcy-court victory is appealed.

If it is absolutely impossible to hire an appellate attorney, and you are forced to file an appellate brief without a lawyer, then you should at least try to find appellate briefs filed in other cases to help you file your own appellate brief.

Saying a Few Words about Private Student Loans

Thanks to the deceptively named Bankruptcy Abuse Prevention and Consumer Protection Act of 2005, private student loans are as difficult to discharge in bankruptcy as federal student loans. For both types of loans, the undue-hardship rule applies.

---

6 Acosta-Conniff v. ECMC (Educational Credit Management Corporation), 536 B.R. 326 (Bankr. M.D. Ala. 2015), *rev'd*, 550 B.R. 557 (M.D. Ala. 2016), *vacated and remanded*, No. 16-12884, 2017 U.S. App. LEXIS 6746 (11th Cir. April 19, 2017) (unpublished decision).

7 Johnson v. Sallie Mae, Inc. and Educational Credit Management Corp., No. 11-23108, Adv. No. 11-6250, 2015 Bankr. LEXIS 525 (Bankr. D. Kan. 2015), *vacated and remanded*, No. 15-2631-JAR2016, 2016 US Dist. LEXIS 27046 (D. Kan. March 1, 2016).

To protect their own interests, the banks and other private student-loan defenders (Sallie Mae, etc.) usually require student borrowers to find cosigners to guarantee their loans. Generally, the cosigner is a parent or other relative.

So remember, even if you discharge a private student loan in bankruptcy, your cosigner is still liable to pay back the loan. And the cosigner, like you, must meet the undue-hardship test if he or she tries to cancel the debt in bankruptcy.

CONCLUDING REMARKS

The student-loan crisis grows worse with each passing month. As the *New York Times* recently noted, 1.1 million student borrowers defaulted on their student loans in 2016[8]—that is an average of three thousand defaults a day!

Bankruptcy judges read the newspapers, and many of them have children or relatives who are overwhelmed by their student loans. I think the judges are beginning to be more sympathetic to "honest but unfortunate" student-loan debtors who acted in good faith and simply cannot pay back their student loans.

Some student borrowers have better cases for bankruptcy discharges than others, but hundreds of thousands of people have decent shots at getting their student loans cancelled through bankruptcy if they just make the effort.

Filing an adversary complaint in a bankruptcy court takes courage, fortitude, and hard work—particularly in gathering the evidence necessary to show a bankruptcy judge that repaying your student loans truly constitutes an undue hardship. And not everyone who seeks relief from student loans through bankruptcy will be successful.

---

8 "The Wrong Move on Student Loans," *New York Times*, April 6, 2017, accessed August 4, 2017, https://www.nytimes.com/2017/04/06/opinion/the-wrong-move-on-student-loans.html?_r=0.

Nevertheless, if you are a student debtor with crushing student loans, you should consider filing for bankruptcy. If after careful thought you determine that you have nothing to lose by filing, then you should file an adversary complaint and fight for relief from oppressive student debt. Others have been successful, and you too might be victorious in a federal bankruptcy court.

Distressed Student-Loan Debtors in the Bankruptcy Courts: What Can You Do to Improve Your Odds of Obtaining a Discharge?

• • •

FEDERAL BANKRUPTCY COURTS HAVE DECIDED a number of cases over the years involving student-loan debtors seeking to wipe out their student loans by filing for bankruptcy. In some cases, the courts have discharged people's student-loan debts, and in other cases, the courts have refused discharges. And the results are not consistent.

For example, in the *Hedlund* case, the Ninth Circuit Court of Appeals granted partial relief to Michael Hedlund, a relatively young law-school graduate who had failed to pass the bar exam.[1] But more recently, in the *Tetzlaff* case, the Eighth Circuit refused to grant relief to an older law-school graduate who had also failed the bar exam and who had a much larger student-loan debt than Mr. Hedlund.[2]

Likewise, an Alabama bankruptcy court refused to discharge student-loan debt owed by a grandfather who had borrowed money back in the 1990s for a degree program he never completed even though the man was living with his wife on $2,000 a month and was broke enough to have his other debts discharged. But another

---

1 Hedlund v. The Educational Resources Institute, Inc. and Pennsylvania Higher Educ. Assistance Agency, 718 F.3d 848 (9th Cir. 2013).

2 Tetzlaff v. Educational Credit Management Corporation (7th Cir. 2015).

Alabama bankruptcy judge discharged the student-loan debt of a woman in her forties who had a pretty good job.

In this essay, I am going to try to give at least some partial answers to two questions: First, when will the DOE and its loan-collection agencies agree to allow a student-loan debtor to discharge student-loan debt in bankruptcy? In other words, how bad does a debtor's financial situation need to be before the DOE will tell a bankruptcy court that it will not oppose the discharge of the student-loan debt? Second, what factors seem to weigh in the debtor's favor when trying to discharge student loans in a bankruptcy-court proceeding?

The DOE and Student-Loan Creditors Oppose Bankruptcy Relief for Nearly Everyone

Regarding the first question, the DOE stated in a July 2015 letter that it would not oppose bankruptcy discharge in certain situations, and it listed eleven factors it would consider when deciding whether or not to agree to a discharge. Those factors are what you might expect and include the debtor's age, health status, and long-term economic prospects. Supposedly, the DOE won't oppose bankruptcy discharges for elderly people living on Social Security or for people with very serious health problems.

In practice, however, the DOE and its debt-collection agencies oppose bankruptcy relief for nearly everyone—even people who are ill and flat broke. The DOE's standard line is that everyone should be forced into a long-term IBRP, even when it is clear the debtor is so poor that that he or she will never be required to pay anything.

For example, in the *Myhre* case, the DOE opposed bankruptcy relief for a quadriplegic man who was gainfully employed but whose expenses exceeded his income because he had to employ a full-time caregiver to feed and dress him and drive him back and forth to work. He's a quadriplegic, for God's sake! Fortunately, the court rejected the DOE's arguments and ruled for Mr. Myhre.[3]

In the *Roth* case, ECMC opposed bankruptcy relief for Jane Roth, a sixty-eight-year-old woman with chronic health problems who was living on less than $800 a month. ECMC argued to put her in a twenty-five-year repayment plan even though it was apparent that Roth would never be able to pay back her student loans.[4]

In the *Abney* case, the DOE opposed relief for Michael Abney, a forty-year-old man who was so poor he couldn't afford a car and rode a bicycle to work. Abney was living on $1,200 a month, and the bankruptcy court ruled that his long-term economic prospects were not likely to improve anytime soon. The DOE insisted on putting him on a long-term repayment plan, but the bankruptcy court sided with Mr. Abney and discharged his student-loan debt.[5]

And in 2016, ECMC persuaded an Illinois bankruptcy court to keep Brenda Butler in a twenty-five-year repayment plan that she won't complete until 2037—forty-two years after she graduated from college. And by the way, Butler was unemployed at the time of her adversary proceeding.[6]

So if you read the DOE's July 2015 letter, just ignore it. In spite of representations by Deputy Assistant Secretary of Education Lynn Mahaffie that the DOE won't oppose bankruptcy relief in some instances, in reality, the DOE doesn't want anyone to get bankruptcy relief. The DOE wants virtually everyone in a twenty- or

---

3 Myhre v. US Department of Education, 503 B. R. 698 (Bankr. W. D. Wis. 2013).

4 Roth v. Educational Credit Management Corporation, 409 B. R. 908 (B.A.P. 9th Cir.2013).

5 Abney v. US Department of Education, 540 B. R. 681 (Bankr. W. D. Mo. 2015).

6 Butler v. Educational Credit Management Corporation, Adv. No. 124-07069, 2016 WL 360697 (Bankr. C. D. Ill. Jan. 27, 2016).

twenty-five-year repayment plan—even if that means people will be saddled with student-loan debt into their nineties.

What You Can Do to Increase Your Odds of Obtaining a Discharge of Your Student-Loan Debt

Now let's turn to the second question: What factors weigh in a person's favor when trying to discharge student-loan debt in a bankruptcy court? There have been several scholarly articles on this topic—Rafael Pardo's work is especially helpful.[7] By and large, the research tells us that people with serious long-term health issues are more likely to obtain relief than people in good health. And it helps to have a competent lawyer.

But a friend of mine has gone to the trouble of calling some of the people who have tried to discharge their student-loan debt in bankruptcy over the past several years, and he's briefed me on what he learned. This is what I've gleaned from these conversations and from my own observations:

1. It helps to prepare well in advance of filing your adversary complaint and to be able to document all student-loan payments that you made and all medical issues that are relevant. In my opinion, it makes sense to file a complaint that contains a lot of detail. Filing a detailed complaint may help educate the bankruptcy judge about your circumstances early in the litigation instead of on the day of trial.

---

7 Rafael I. Pardo, "The Undue Hardship Thicket: On Access to Justice, Procedural Noncompliance, and Pollutive Litigation in Bankruptcy," *Florida Law Review* 66, no. 6 (2014): 2101-2178; Rafael I. Pardo and Michelle R. Lacey, "The Real Student Loan Scandal: Undue Hardship Discharge Litigation," *American Bankruptcy Law Journal* 83 (2009): 179-236; Rafael I. Pardo, "Illness and Inability to Repay: The Role of Debtor Health in the Discharge of Educational Debt," *Florida State University Law Review* 35 (2008): 505-524.

2. You should be wary of agreeing to anything the creditor's attorney suggests, especially if you are representing yourself and don't have an attorney. For example, in a recent case, a DOE attorney persuaded a debtor to agree that it would not be an undue hardship to pay back his student loans, even though the guy was in bankruptcy for that very reason. The debtor wasn't aware that by agreeing to what the attorney suggested, he had lost his case. And in fact, case law would have supported an argument that indeed it would have been an undue hardship to repay his student loans.

3. It is good to have an attorney, but your attorney must know the law—especially the recent cases that have ruled more compassionately toward student-loan debtors. In one recent case—a real heartbreaker—an unemployed woman in her forties, who had made good-faith efforts to pay her student loans for twenty years, got locked into a twenty-five-year repayment plan that will not conclude until she is in her sixties.[8] Apparently, the judge was never made aware that courts have granted relief to several people within the last two years whose financial situations were far better than hers.

Whether or not you have an attorney, you must know the law. In particular, you need to find out how the federal circuit court for your jurisdiction has ruled in student-loan bankruptcy cases.

You should be aware that most judges won't require you to have lived on bread and water in order to qualify for a discharge of your student loans. For example, several courts have rejected creditors' arguments that student-loan debtors are not living frugally if they have a cell phone, an Internet account, or a pet or have incurred

---

8 Butler v. Educational Credit Management Corporation, Case No. 14-71585, Chapter 7, Adv. No. 14-07069, 2016 Bankr. LEXIS 245 (Bankr. C.D. Ill. 2016).

some other discretionary expense. If your creditor makes that argument (and it will), it would be good to be able to cite those cases.[9]

You should be able to tell the judge that several courts in the *Brunner* jurisdictions have refused to interpret the *Brunner* test harshly, and you should point out those cases to your judge in your trial brief.

Finally, you should know the cases in which judges have refused to force distressed student-loan debtors into twenty-five-year repayment plans. Several courts have pointed out the psychological stress that a long-term repayment plan can have on a person (*Abney, Fern,* and *Lamento*).[10] It is essential for you to be able to educate your judge about court decisions that have rejected the creditors' stock argument, which is to force everyone into long-term repayment plans.

---

9 Educational Credit Management Corporation v. Frushour, 433 F.3d 393, 401 (4th Cir. 2005) (fact that debtor had internet service and cable television did not disqualify her from obtaining an undue hardship bankruptcy discharge but ruling for creditor on other grounds); Educational Credit Management Corporation v. Kelly, 312 B.R. 200, 207 (B.A.P. 1st Cir. 2004) (affirming bankruptcy court's decision that internet and cable television were consistent with minimal standard of living); McDowell v. Educational Credit Management Corporation, 549 B.R. 744, 767 (Bankr. D. Idaho 2016) ("Given the other demands in her life and Plaintiff's health concerns, a modest expense for eating out is not inappropriate in measuring a minimal standard of living); Myhre v. US Department of Education, 503 B.R. 698, 704 (Bankr. W.D. Wis. 2013) (cable access for TV and internet are necessary for quadriplegic to maintain minimal standard of living); Shaffer v. US Department of Education, Adversary No. 10–30109, 2011 WL 6010240,*3 (Bank. S.D. Iowa 2011), aff'd, 481 B.R. 15 (8th Cir. 2012) (debtor's entertainment expense of $75 a month and pet care expenses were consistent with frugal lifestyle); Walker v. Sallie Mae Servicing Corporation, 406 B.R. 840, 861 (Bankr. D. Minn. 2009) (construction of screened deck on family home was reasonable).

10 Abney v. US Department of Education, 540 B. R. 681 (Bankr. W. D. Mo. 2015); Fern v. FedLoan Servicing, 553 B. R. 362 (Bankr. N. D. Iowa 2016), *affirmed,* 563 B. R. 1 (B.A.P. 8th Cir. 2017); Lamento v. US Department of Education, 520 B. R. 667 (Bankr. N. D. Ohio 2014).

Your Judge May Be Sympathetic

Finally, you should know that there are factors at work that are beyond a student-loan debtor's control—such as the temperament of the bankruptcy judge. I think many of these judges are inclined to be sympathetic toward student-loan debtors—many of whom have been crushed not by their loans but by the creditors' collection fees and accruing interest. I believe many of these judges want to help you. After all, the bankruptcy judges know that the bankruptcy courts exist in order to give honest but unfortunate debtors fresh starts.

And it is also evident that some bankruptcy judges are willing to do a lot of research and to write impressively reasoned decisions in favor of student-loan debtors. The judge in *Acosta-Conniff v. ECMC*,[11] the judge in *Johnson v. Sallie Mae*,[12] and the judge in *Abney v. Department of Education*[13] went to a lot of trouble to write decisions in favor of student-loan debtors that would have a good chance of being upheld by the appellate courts in the event their opinions were appealed. But you can help your judge tremendously if you can point out cases in your trial brief that have been decided recently in favor of student-loan debtors whose cases are similar to yours.

Trying to discharge your student loans in bankruptcy is a daunting challenge. You will be opposed by squadrons of creditors' attorneys who know the law and who show no mercy. And if you win, the

---

11 Acosta-Conniff v. ECMC (Educational Credit Management Corporation), 536 B.R. 326 (Bankr. M.D. Ala. 2015), *rev'd*, 550 B.R. 557 (M.D. Ala. 2016), *vacated and remanded*, No. 16-12884, 2017 U.S. App. LEXIS 6746 (11th Cir. April 19, 2017) (unpublished decision).

12 Johnson v. Sallie Mae, Inc. and Educational Credit Management Corp., No. 11-23108, Adv. No. 11-6250, 2015 Bankr. LEXIS 525 (Bankr. D. Kan. 2015), *vacated and remanded*, No. 15-2631-JAR2016, 2016 US Dist. LEXIS 27046 (D. Kan. March 1, 2016).

13 Abney v. US Department of Education, 540 B. R. 681 (Bankr. W. D. Mo. 2015).

creditors are likely to appeal, hoping they will wear you down and you will simply give up.

But I believe in my heart that the winds of justice are blowing through the bankruptcy courts and that many bankruptcy judges are willing to help you if you have a good case. But to repeat myself, you will help your judge tremendously if you educate him or her about recent favorable decisions—including *Roth, Krieger,* and more than a dozen others.[14] If you are a distressed student-loan debtor with a reasonable case for discharge, go to the bankruptcy court, and plead for justice. You have a good chance of getting the justice you deserve.

As they sometimes say in the Southwest, *vaya con Dios.* Go with God.

---

14 Roth v. Educational Credit Management Corporation, 409 B. R. 908 (B.A.P. 9th Cir. 2013); Krieger v. Educational Credit Management Corp., 713 F.3d 882 (7th Cir. 2013).

BIBLIOGRAPHY

Abney v. US Department of Education. 540 B. R. 681 (Bank. W.D. Mo. 2015).

Acosta-Conniff v. ECMC (Educational Credit Management Corporation), 536 B.R. 326 (Bankr. M.D. Ala. 2015), *rev'd*, 550 B.R. 557 (M.D. Ala. 2016), *vacated and remanded*, No. 16-12884, 2017 U.S. App. LEXIS 6746 (11th Cir. April 19, 2017) (unpublished decision).

Akers, Beth, and Matthew Chingos. *Game of Loans: The Rhetoric and Reality of Student Debt.* Princeton, NJ: Princeton University Press, 2016.

Andriotis, Annamaria. "Debt Relief for Students Snarls Market for Their Loans." *Wall Street Journal*, September 23, 2015, accessed August 7, 2017, https://www.wsj.com/articles/debt-relief-is-snarling-the-market-for-student-loans-1443035071.

Ashbrook, Tom. "Parents on the Hook for Student Loans." *NPR Onpoint* (podcast), April 26, 2017. http://www.wbur.org/onpoint/2017/04/26/parents-student-loans.

Baum, Sandy. *Student Debt: Rhetoric and Realities of Higher Education Financing.* New York: Palgrave-MacMillan, 2016.

Berman, Jillian. "When Your Social Security Check Disappears Because of an Old Student Loan." *MarketWatch*, June 25, 2015. http://www.marketwatch.com/story/when-your-social-security-check-disappears-because-of-an-old-student-loan-2015-06-25.

Boesler, Mathew. "More College Grads Finding Work, But Not in the Best Jobs." April 7, 2016. https://www.bloomberg.com/news/articles/2016-04-07/more-college-grads-finding-work-but-not-in-the-best-jobs.

Brown, Meta, Haughwout, Andrew, Lee, Donghoon, Mabutas, Maricar, and van der Klaauw, Wilbert. "Grading Student Loans." *Liberty Street Economics* (blog), May 5, 2012, accessed August 5, 2017, http://libertystreeteconomics.newyorkfed.org/2012/03/grading-student-loans.htmlhttp://libertystreeteconomics.newyorkfed.org/2012/03/grading-student-loans.html.

Bruner-Halteman v. Educational Credit Management Corp. Case No. 12-324-HDH-13. ADV. No. 14-03041, 2016 WL 1427085 (Bankr. N.D. Tex. 2016).

Brunner v. New York State Higher Educ. Services Corp., 831 F.2d 395, 396 (2d Cir. 1987).

Butler v. Educational Credit Management Corp. Adv. No. 124-07069. 2016 WL 360697. (Bankr. C.D. Ill. Jan. 27, 2016).

Campos, Paul. *Don't Go To Law School (Unless)*. Lexington, KY: CreateSpace Independent Publishing Platform, 2012.

Case, Anne, and Angus Deaton. "Rising Morbidity and Mortality in Midlife among White Non-Hispanic Americans in the 21st Century," *PNAS* 112, no. 49 (December 2015): 15078–15083. http://www.pnas.org/content/early/2015/10/29/1518393112.full.pdf.

Carey, Kevin. "Lend With a Smile, Collect With a Fist." *New York Times*, November 29, 2015, accessed August 6, 2017, https://www.

nytimes.com/2015/11/29/upshot/student-debt-in-america-lend-with-a-smile-collect-with-a-fist.html.

Chakrabarti, Rajashri, Andrew Haughwout, Donghoon Lee, Joelle Scally, and Wilbert van der Klaauw. "At the N.Y. Fed: Press Briefing on Household Borrowing with Close-Up on Student Debt." *Liberty Street Economics* (blog), April 3, 2017. http://libertystreeteconomics.newyorkfed.org/2017/04/at-the-ny-fed-press-briefing-on-household-borrowing-with-close-up-on-student-debt.html.

Citizens Bank. "Millennial College Graduates with Student Loans Now Spending Nearly One-Fifth of Their Annual Salaries on Student Loan Repayments." April 7, 2016. http://investor.citizensbank.com/about-us/newsroom/latest-news/2016/2016-04-07-140336028.aspx.

Conner v. US Department of Education. Case No. 15-1-541, 2016 WL 1178264 (E.D. Mich. March 28, 2016).

Corkery, Michael, and Stacy Cowley. "Household Debt Makes a Comeback in the U.S." *New York Times*, May 17, 2017, accessed August 5, 2017, https://www.nytimes.com/2017/05/17/business/dealbook/household-debt-united-states.html?_r=0.

Douglas-Gabriel, Danielle. "It's going to cost taxpayers $108 billion to help student loan borrowers." *Washington Post*, November 30, 2016, accessed August 6, 2017, https://www.washingtonpost.com/news/grade-point/wp/2016/11/30/its-going-to-cost-tax-payers-108-billion-to-help-student-loan-borrowers/?

Douglas-Gabriel, Danielle. "It's Time to Reform the Financial Arm of the Education Department, Report Says." *Washington Post*,

May 16, 2017, accessed August 4, 2017, www.washingtonpost.com/news/grade-point/wp/2017/05/16/its-time-to-reform-the-financial-arm-of-the-education-department-report-says/?

Educational Credit Management Corporation v. Frushour, 433 F.3d 393 (4th Cir. 2005).

Educational Credit Management Corporation v. Kelly, 312 B.R. 200 (B.A.P. 1st Cir. 2004).

Educational Credit Management Corporation v. Kelly, No. C11–1263RSL, 2012 WL 1378725 (W.D. Wash. 2012), *reversed*, 594 Fed. App. 413 (9th Cir. 2015) (unpublished decision).

Educational Credit Management Corporation v. Nys, 446 F.3d 938 (9th Cir. 2006).

Educational Credit Management Corp. v. Polleys. 356 F.3d 1302 (10th Cir. 2004).

Fain, Paul. "Feds' Data Error Inflated Loan Repayment Rates on the College Scoreboard." *Inside Higher Ed*, January 16, 2017, accessed August 6, 2017, https://www.insidehighered.com/news/2017/01/16/feds-data-error-inflated-loan-repayment-rates-college-scorecard.

Federal Reserve Bank of New York. *The Labor Market for Recent College Graduates* (2016). https://www.newyorkfed.org/research/college-labor-market/index.html.

Fern v. FedLoan Servicing, 553 B. R. 362 (Bankr. N. D. Iowa 2016), *aff'd*, 563 B. R. 1 (B.A.P. 8th Cir. 2017).

Fern v. FedLoan Servicing. 563 B. R. 1 (B.A.P. 8th Cir. 2017).

Gillespie, Patrick. "University of Phoenix Has Lost Half Its Students." *CNN Money*, March 25, 2015, accessed August 7, 2017. http://money.cnn.com/2015/03/25/investing/university-of-phoenix-apollo-earnings-tank/.

Harris, Adam. "Top Federal Student-Aid Official Resigns Over Congressional Testimony." *Chronicle of Higher Education*, May 24, 2017, accessed August 7, 2017. http://www.chronicle.com/blogs/ticker/top-federal-student-aid-official-resigns-over-congressional-testimony/118615.

Hedlund v. The Educational Resources Institute., Inc. and Pennsylvania Higher Education Assistance Agency, 718 F.3d 848 (9th Cir. 2013).

Hempstead, Katherine A., and Julie A. Phillips. "Rising Suicide among Adults Aged 40–64 Years: The Role of Job and Financial Circumstances." *American Journal of Preventive Medicine* 84, no. 5 (2015): 491–500. http://www.ajpmonline.org/article/S0749-3797(14)00662-X/pdf.

Iuliano, Jason. "An Empirical Assessment of Student Loan Discharge and the Undue Hardship Standard." *American Bankruptcy Law Journal* 86 (2012): 495-525.

Johnson v. Sallie Mae, Inc. and Educational Credit Management Corp. No. 11-23108. Adv. No. 11-6250. 2015 Bankr. LEXIS 525 (Bankr. D. Kan. 2015), *vacated and remanded*, No. 15-2631-JAR2016. 2016 US Dist. LEXIS 27046 (D. Kan. March 1, 2016).

Johnson v. US Department of Education. 541 B. R. 750 (Bankr. N. D. Ala. 2015).

Kelly v. Sallie Mae, Inc. and Educational Credit Management Corporation. 594 Fed. App. 413 (9th Cir. 2015).

Kezar, Korri. "Why a Dallas Restaurant Company's Bankruptcy Is Part of a Trend." WFAA.com, August 10, 2016, accessed August 5, 2017, http://www.wfaa.com/news/local/dallas-county/ why-a-dallas-restaurant-companys-bankruptcy-is-part-of-a-trend/293988701?

Kelchen, Robert. "How much do for-profit colleges rely on federal funds?" *Brown Center Chalkboard* (blog), January 11, 2017, accessed August 6, 2017, https://www.brookings.edu/blog/brown-center-chalkboard/2017/01/11/how-much-do-for-profit-colleges-rely-on-federal-funds/.

Kitroeff, Natalie. "Loan Monitor Is Accused of Ruthless Tactics on Student Debt." *New York Times*, January 1, 2014, accessed August 4, 2017. http://www.nytimes.com/2014/01/02/us/loan-monitor-is-accused-of-ruthless-tactics-on-student-debt.html?_r=0.

Kolata, Gina. "Deaths Rates Rising Middle-Aged White Americans, Study Finds." *New York Times*, November 3, 2015, accessed August 7, 2017. https://www.nytimes.com/2015/11/03/health/death-rates-rising-for-middle-aged-white-americans-study-finds.html

Krieger v. Educational Credit Management Corporation. 713 F.3d 882 (7th Cir. 2013).

Lamento v. US Department of Education. 520 B. R. 667 (Bankr, N.D. Ohio 2014).

Lieber, Ron. "Placing the Blame as Students Are Buried in Debt." *New York Times*, May 28, 2010, accessed August 7, 2017. http://www.nytimes.com/2010/05/29/your-money/student-loans/29money.html.

Lockhart v. United States. 546 US 142. 126 S. Ct. 699 (2005).

Looney, Adam, and Constantine Yannelis. *A Crisis in Student Loans? How Changes in the Characteristics of Borrowers and in the Institutions They Attended Contributed to Rising Default Rates.* Washington, DC: Brookings Institution, 2015). https://www.brookings.edu/bpea-articles/a-crisis-in-student-loans-how-changes-in-the-characteristics-of-borrowers-and-in-the-institutions-they-at-tended-contributed-to-rising-loan-defaults/.

Magno v. The College Network, Inc. 204 Cal. Rptr. 3d 829 (Cal. Ct. App. 2016).

McDowell v. Educational Credit Management Corporation, 549 B.R. 744 (Bankr. D. Idaho 2016).

McEntee, Kyle. "Law Grads Still Face Tough a Job Market." *Bloomberg Law*, May 4, 2016, accessed August 7, 2017. https://bol.bna.com/law-grads-still-face-a-tough-job-market/.

McKay, Betsy. "The Death Rate Is Rising for Middle-Aged Whites." *Wall Street Journal*, November 3, 2015, August 7, 2017. http://www.wsj.com/articles/the-death-rate-is-rising-for-middle-aged-whites-1446499495.

Mitchell, Josh. "The U.S. Makes It Easy for Parents to Get College Loans—Repaying Them Is Another Story." *Wall Street Journal*, April 24, 2017, accessed August 6, 2017. https://www.wsj.com/

articles/the-u-s-makes-it-easy-for-parents-to-get-college-loan-srepaying-them-is-another-story-1493047388.

————. "Student-Debt Forgiveness Plans Skyrocket, Raising Fears Over Costs, Higher Tuition," *Wall Street Journal*, April 22, 2014, accessed August 7, 2017, https://www.wsj.com/articles/plans-that-forgive-student-debt-skyrocket-raising-fears-over-costs-1398126083.

Morgan v. Sanford Brown Institute. 137 A.3d 1168 (N. J. 2016).

Murray v. Educational Credit Management Corporation, 563 B.R. 52 (Bankr. D. Kan. 2016).

Myhre v. US Department of Education. 503 B. R. 698 (Bank. W.D. Wis. 2013).

Narayanswamy, Anu, Cameron, Darla, and Matea Gold, Matea. "How much money is behind each campaign?" *Washington Post*, February 1, 2017, accessed August 3, 2017, https://www.washingtonpost.com/graphics/politics/2016-election/campaign-finance/.

Nasiripour, Shahien. "Education Department Secretly Reappoints Top Official Accused of Harming Students." *Huffington Post*, May 7, 2016, Accessed August 7, 2017. http://www.huffingtonpost.com/entry/education-dept-student-loans_us_5728fdebe4b0bc9cb044dc16.

National Association of Student Financial Aid Administrators. *Improving Oversight and Transparency at the US Department of Education's Financial Aid: NASFAA's Recommendations.* May 2017. https://www.nasfaa.org/uploads/documents/NASFAA_FSA_Report.pdf.

New York Times. "Death among Middle Aged Whites." November 5, 2015.

New York Times. "The Wrong Move on Student Loans." April 6, 2017. https://www.nytimes.com/2017/04/06/opinion/the-wrong-move-on-student-loans.html?_r=0.

New York Times. "Why Student Debtors Go Unrescued." October 7, 2015, accessed August 6, 2017. http://www.nytimes.com/2015/10/07/opinion/why-student-debtors-go-unrescued.html?_r=0.

Pardo, Rafael I. "Illness and Inability to Repay: The Role of Debtor Health in the Discharge of Educational Debt." *Florida State University Law Review* 35 (2008): 505-524.

Pardo, Rafael I. "The Undue Hardship Thicket: On Access to Justice, Procedure Noncompliance, and Pollutive Litigation in Bankruptcy." *Florida Law Review* 66, no. 6 (2014): 2101-2178.

Pardo, Rafael I. and Lacey, Michelle R. "The Real Student Loan Scandal: Undue Hardship Discharge Litigation." *American Bankruptcy Law Journal* 83 (2009): 179-236.

Precht v. US Department of Education. AD PRO 15-01167-RGM (Bankr. E.D. Va. Feb. 11, 2016) (Consent Order).

Roth v. Educational Credit Management Corporation, 490 B. R. 908 (B.A.P. 9th Cir. 2013).

Scheiber, Noam. "An Expensive Law Degree and No Place to Use It." *New York Times,* June 17, 2016, accessed August 7, 2017. http://

www.nytimes.com/2016/06/19/business/dealbook/an-expensive-law-degree-and-no-place-to-use-it.html?_r=0.

Schlesinger, Jill. "Looking for the Next Bubble." *Chicago Tribune*, August 24, 2016, accessed August 4, 2017. http://www.chicago-tribune.com/business/.

Scott-Clayton, Judith, and Jing Li. "Black-White Disparity in Student Loan Debt More than Triples after Graduation." *Evidence Speaks Reports* 2, no. 3 (October 2016): https://www.brookings.edu/research/black-white-disparity-in-student-loan-debt-more-than-triples-after-graduation/.

Scott v. US Department of Education. 417 B. R. 623 (Bankr. W. D. Wash. 2009).

Segal, David. "High Debt and Falling Demand Trap New Vets." *New York Times*, February 23, 2013, accessed August 7, 2017. http://www.nytimes.com/2013/02/24/business/high-debt-and-falling-demand-trap-new-veterinarians.html.

Shaffer v. US Department of Education, Adversary No. 10–30109, 2011 WL 6010240 (Bankr. S.D. Iowa 2011), aff'd, 481 B.R. 15 (8th Cir. 2012).

Shaffer v. US Department of Education. 481 B. R. 15 (8th Cir. 2012).

Shireman, Robert, and Tariq Habash. *Have Student Loan Guaranty Agencies Lost Their Way?* The Century Foundation, September 29, 2016, accessed August 5, 2017, https://tcf.org/content/report/student-loan-guaranty-agencies-lost-way/.

Stevenson v. Educational Credit Management Corp. 463 B. R. 586 (Bankr. D. Mass. 2011), *aff'd*, 475 B. R. 286 (D. Mass. 2012).

Stratford, Michael. "The New College Scorecard." *Inside Higher Ed*, September 14, 2015, accessed August 5, 2017. https://www.insidehighered.com/news/2015/09/14/obama-administration-publishes-new-college-earnings-loan-repayment-data.

Tergesen, Anne. "Six Common Mistakes People Make with Their Student Loans." *Wall Street Journal*, September 12, 2016, accessed August 7, 2017. http://www.wsj.com/articles/six-common-mistakes-people-make-with-their-student-loans-1473645782.

Tetzlaff v. Educational Credit Management Corporation (7th Cir. 2015).

Theis, Michael. "Italian Restaurant Chain Again Files for Bankruptcy." *Austin Business Journal*, July 27, 2016. http://www.bizjournals.com/austin/news/2016/07/27/italian-restaurant-chain-files-again-for.html.

Thielen, Amy. "Declines at For-Profit Colleges Take a Big Toll on Their Stocks." *The Street*, May 8, 2015 (blog), accessed August 7, 2017. https://www.thestreet.com/story/13144238/1/decline-in-for-profit-colleges-takes-a-big-toll-on-their-stocks.html.

Website for Elizabeth Warren. "McCaskill-Warren GAO Report Shows Shocking Increase in Student Loan Debt among Seniors." December 20, 2016. https://www.warren.senate.gov/?p=press_release&id=1331.

Website for John Delaney. "Delaney and Katko File Legislation to Help Americans Struggling with Student Loan Debt." May 5,

2017. https://delaney.house.gov/news/press-releases/delaney-and-katko-file-legislation-to-help-americans-struggling-with-student.

White, Alan. "Foreclosure Crisis Update." *Credit Slip*, April 5, 2017 (blog), accessed August 7, 2017. http://www.creditslips.org/creditslips/2017/04/foreclosure-crisis-update.html?

Woodhouse, Kellie. "Discounting Grows Again." *Inside Higher Ed*, August 25, 2015, accessed August 5, 2017, https://www.insidehighered.com/news/2015/08/25/tuition-discounting-grows-private-colleges-and-universities.

US Government Accountability Office. *Older Americans: Inability to Repay Student Loans May Affect Financial Security of a Small Percentage of Borrowers*. Washington, DC: Government Accountability Office. http://www.gao.gov/products/GAO-14-866T.

US Government Accountability Office. *Social Security Offsets: Improvement to Program Design Could Better Assist Older Student Borrowers with Obtaining Permitted Relief.* (Washington, DC: December 2016). http://www.gao.gov/assets/690/681722.pdf, 11.

US Department of Education. "US Department of Education Takes Further Steps to Protect Students from Predatory Higher Education Institutions." March 11, 2016. http://www.ed.gov/news/press-releases/us-department-education-takes-further-steps-protect-students-predatory-higher-education-institutions?

Walker v. Sallie Mae Servicing Corporation, 406 B.R. 840, 861 (Bankr. D. Minn. 2009).

Yale News. "Yale Financial Aid Budget Will Meet Term Bill Increase." March 9, 2016, accessed August 5, 2017, http://news.yale. edu/2016/03/09/yale-financial-aid-budget-will-meet-term-bill-increase.

Yarbrough, Ann. "Bar Exam Pass Rate Dips to 32-Year Low." *California Bar Journal* (December 2016). http://www.calbarjournal.com/December2016/TopHeadlines/TH2.aspx.

83081965R00089

Made in the USA
Columbia, SC
08 December 2017